POETRY FROM CRESCENT MOON

William Shakespeare: *The Sonnets*
edited, with an introduction by Mark Tuley

William Shakespeare: *Complete Poems*
edited and introduced by Mark Tuley

Elizabethan Sonnet Cycles
edited and introduced by Mark Tuley

Edmund Spenser: *Heavenly Love: Selected Poems*
selected and introduced by Teresa Page

Edmund Spenser: *Amoretti*
edited by Teresa Page

Robert Herrick: *Delight In Disorder: Selected Poems*
edited and introduced by M.K. Pace

Sir Thomas Wyatt: *Love For Love: Selected Poems*
selected and introduced by Louise Cooper

John Donne: *Air and Angels: Selected Poems*
selected and introduced by A.H. Ninham

D.H. Lawrence: *Being Alive: Selected Poems*
edited with an introduction by Margaret Elvy

D.H. Lawrence: Symbolic Landscapes
by Jane Foster

D.H. Lawrence: Infinite Sensual Violence
by M.K. Pace

Percy Bysshe Shelley: *Paradise of Golden Lights: Selected Poems*
selected and introduced by Charlotte Greene

Thomas Hardy: *Her Haunting Ground: Selected Poems*
edited, with an introduction by A.H. Ninham

Sexing Hardy: Thomas Hardy and Feminism
by Margaret Elvy

Emily Bronte: *Darkness and Glory: Selected Poems*
selected and introduced by Miriam Chalk

John Keats: *Bright Star: Selected Poems*
edited with an introduction by Miriam Chalk

John Keats: *Poems of 1820*
edited with an introduction by Miriam Chalk

Henry Vaughan: *A Great Ring of Pure and Endless Light: Selected Poems*
selected and introduced by A.H. Ninham

The Crescent Moon Book of Love Poetry
edited by Louise Cooper

The Crescent Moon Book of Mystical Poetry in English
edited by Carol Appleby

The Crescent Moon Book of Nature Poetry From Langland to Lawrence
edited by Margaret Elvy

The Crescent Moon Book of Metaphysical Poetry
edited and introduced by Charlotte Greene

The Crescent Moon Book of Elizabethan Love Poetry
edited and introduced by Carol Appleby

The Crescent Moon Book of Romantic Poetry
edited and introduced by L.M. Poole

Peter Redgrove: Here Comes the Flood
by Jeremy Mark Robinson

Sex-Magic-Poetry-Cornwall: A Flood of Poems
by Peter Redgrove, edited with an essay by Jeremy Mark Robinson

Brigitte's Blue Heart
by Jeremy Reed

Claudia Schiffer's Red Shoes
by Jeremy Reed

By-Blows: Uncollected Poems
by D.J. Enright

Dante: *Selections From the Vita Nuova*
translated by Thomas Okey

Arthur Rimbaud: *Selected Poems*
edited and translated by Andrew Jary

Arthur Rimbaud: *A Season in Hell*
edited and translated by Andrew Jary

Friedrich Hölderlin: *Hölderlin's Songs of Light: Selected Poems*
translated by Michael Hamburger

Rainer Maria Rilke: *Dance the Orange:* Selected Poems
translated by Michael Hamburger

German Romantic Poetry: Goethe, Novalis, Heine, Hölderlin
by Carol Appleby

Arseny Tarkovsky: *Life, Life: Selected Poems*
translated by Virginia Rounding

Emily Dickinson: *Wild Nights: Selected Poems*
selected and introduced by Miriam Chalk

Petrarch, Dante and the Troubadours

The Religion of Love and Poetry

Petrarch, Dante and the Troubadours:
The Religion of Love and Poetry

Jeremy Mark Robinson

CRESCENT MOON

CRESCENT MOON PUBLISHING
P.O. Box 1312, Maidstone
Kent, ME14 5XU
Great Britain
ww.crmoon.com

First published 1993. This edition 2020.

Set in Book Antiqua 10 on 14pt.
Designed by Radiance Graphics.

British Library Cataloguing in Publication data

ISBN-13 9781861717801 (Pbk)
ISBN-13 9781861717887 (Hbk)

CONTENTS

ACKNOWLEDGEMENTS

Acknowledgements are due to the publishers of Francesco Petrarch's poetry, in particular Harvard University Press, Cambridge, MA, for the *Rime Sparse*; to Oxford University Press for Dante's *Vita Nuova* and *Selections from the Canzoniere*; also for books by Peter Dronke, Linda M. Paterson and Kenhelm Foster; to Cambridge University Press for L.T. Topsfield's *Troubadours and Love*; to Manchester University Press for Bernard O'Donoghue's *The Courtly Love Tradition,* Stephen Minta's *Petrarch and Petrarchism,* and *Petrarch's Selected Poems*; to Edinburgh University Press for Alan R. Press's *Anthology of Troubadour Lyric Poetry*; to Penguin for Dante's *Paradise*; to all other publishers and authors cited in the text.

A NOTE ON TEXTS

Robert M. Durling's translations of Francesco Petrarch's poetry have been used for Petrarch's texts; Mark Musa's translation of Dante has been used for the *Vita Nuova* and the *Divine Comedy*; Alan R. Press's and L.T. Topsfield's translation of troubadour lyrics have been used; other translations are noted in the text and Notes.

Marie Spartali Stillman, The First Meeting of Petrarch and Laura de Sade

Henry Holiday, Dante and Beatrice

INTRODUCTION

ðૐ

Francesco Petrarch (Francesco Petrarca, July 20, 1304 - July 19, 1374) is the supreme poet of love in the Western tradition, alongside poets such as Sappho and William Shakespeare. Francesco Petrarch is also the Renaissance artist and humanist par excellence. Petrarchism, an enormously influential literary movement, is regarded as the longest poetic tradition in the Occident,[1] and Petrarch has influenced poets such as Maurice Scève, Sir Thomas Wyatt, Torquato Tasso, Edmund Spenser, Michael Drayton, Joachim Du Bellay, Pierre de Ronsard, Rainer Maria Rilke and Robert Graves, among hundreds of others.

Francesco Petrarch is also called the first modernist: his poetic persona is an early, modern version of one of those now familiar solitary, bourgeois, modern outsiders, the kind found in the work of Jean-Paul Sartre, Knut Hamsun, André Gide, Albert Camus and Arthur Rimbaud.

Francesco Petrarch is a poet's poet, an artist who tried to make art in the purest fashion, who burned brightly for his art. He is one of the first poets to exalt the individual in the way we recognize as modern, and Petrarch's ruthless self-analysis seems wholly in tune with that of, say, Arthur Rimbaud, Julia Kristeva, Paul Valéry, Lawrence Durrell or Virginia Woolf.

But it is as a love poet that Francesco Petrarch is celebrated – as a love poet rather than a rhetorician, humanist or philosopher (although his work in those areas is very important). Petrarch's *Canzoniere*, often also known as the *Rime Sparse*, lies at the heart of his achievement: it comprises 366 poems about love, written in Italian and worked on right up until Petrarch's death in 1374. Petrarch's other major works included *Secretum, Triumphs, Africa, De Vita Solitaria,* and his letters.

Love rules, and Francesco Petrarch remains so popular partly because of his love poetry, because he writes so well about love, because he flatters the reader's received notions of love, because most critics (the people who exalt Petrarch in critical writings) are male, and Petrarch's philosophy of love is masculinist and patriarchal. Petrarch celebrates mainly masculine ideas of love, sex, seduction and romance. He trades on desire, and desire is at the heart of Western culture (expressed in movies, pop songs, advertizing, novels, magazines, radio shows, TV sit coms, fashion, etc). The desire is for the unattainable – variously imagined to be the distant but beautiful woman, the Holy Grail, the ideal love, Heaven (and, more recently, in Western, capitalist societies, embodied in consumerism, such as an expensive new car, a gorgeous, artificially-enhanced body, celebrity status, and a Hollywood penthouse with swimming pools, tennis courts and a garage full of gleaming vehicles, or, so often in contemporary movies, a suitcase stuffed full of dollars).

The focus of the quest in Francesco Petrarch's *Rime Sparse* is Laura de Sade, the beloved woman (she was probably Laura de Noves, wife of the Count Hugues de Sade. As modern commentators can't resist pointing out, Laura's husband was an ancestor of the Marquis de Sade, further embedding Petrarch in the *avant garde* and progressive literary tradition of Europe).

We should remind ourselves before going further, that outside of the *Rime Sparse,* Petrarch could be as chauvinistic as other writers in the mediæval era in some of his views. In the *Familiares,* he said: '[r]esort to women, without which

I had at times thought I could not live, I now fear worse than death;

and though I am often disturbed by the sharpest of temptation, yet when there comes into my mind what woman is, all temptation immediately departs. (X, V, 100)

In many letters, Francesco Petrarch painted a picture of domestic hell – wailing babies, sleepless nights and the 'endless company of women' (*Seniles* XIV, iv. 1035). Petrarch's chauvinism (verging on misogynism) must be kept in mind as one journeys through the adulation of women in the *Rime Sparse*. The chauvinism and distrust of women is of his time, of course, and can be found in many other works of the same period, but that doesn't not excuse it.[2]

Everything that men say about love, Francesco Petrarch provides. He delivers, like Dante Alighieri or William Shakespeare, exactly what consumers want. Petrarch's poems are made for an audience that is largely, if not wholly, male. And if not exclusively male, it is thoroughly patriarchal, and certainly highly educated and well-off.

I concentrate here on the *Rime Sparse*, not on the extraordinary amount of other works: the *Triumphs, Africa,* verse epistles, biographies, allegorical ecologues and hundreds of letters. Francesco Petrarch is portrayed here as a love poet; he is set within the (Western) love poetry tradition. Petrarch took much from the troubadours, so courtly love ethics, myths and morals of courtly love are studied first, followed by the beloved women in the works of Dante Alighieri and Petrarch.

In discussing Petrarch and Dante I refer to the authors and their works, but often really mean 'the Dante-poet' or 'the Petrarch-poet', or, to put it another way, 'the poet in Dante's poem' or 'the poet in Petrarch's poem'.

Because Petrarch and Dante are far too sophisticated as writers to be identified transparently with the selfs or I's in their works. When Petrarch or Dante writes 'I' or 'me', that 'I' or 'me' is a poetic self, not the real person. And not just a poetic 'I', but a self within a highly stylized and artificial literary form, a poem. And not a poem by just anybody, but a poem by two incredibly intelligent, highly-educated and acutely self-conscious artists.

Francesco Petrarch emerges as the poet who is the apotheosis of the courtly love tradition, and his *Canzoniere* is the supreme example of the troubadour ethic. At the same time, the *Canzoniere* is a decadent text, falling into self-parody and too sweetly refined artifice. The power of Petrarch's work is even so undeniable. Articles and magazines and quarterlies and journals abound which deal with Petrarch and aspects of his poetry, philosophy and rhetoric: *Convivium, Journal of the History of Ideas, Modern Language Notes, Studies in Philology. Giornala storico del la letteratura itallana, Pacific Coast Philology, Italian Philological Quarterly, Cultura Neolatina, Forum Italicum, Dante Studies, Yearbook of Italian Studies, Lettere Italiane, Italian Quarterly, Italianistica, Italia medioevale et umanistica, Enciclopedia Dantesca, Diacritics, Journal of Medieval and Renaissance Studies, Romance Notes* and *Renaissance and Reformation*.

The *Canzoniere* comprises 366 poems. Most are sonnets – the famous Petrarchan sonnet form, so influential on European poetry. It consists 14 lines, with a rime scheme of abbaabba (the 8 lines of the octave), and cdecde, cdcdcd, cddcdd or cddece (for the 6 lines of the sestet). In the *Canzoniere*, there are hundreds of sonnets, 29 *canzoni* (songs), 7 *ballate* (ballads), 9 *sestine* and 4 *madrigali*. As well as sonnets, there are songs or *canzone*, which are longer lyrical pieces, though still with strict rime schemes and line lengths.

The text of the *Rime Sparse* used in this study is that of Robert M. Durling's 1976 translation. Francesco Petrarch is a superbly musical lyrical poet, and his forms, wordplay, rhymes, patterns, shapes and ideas are difficult to render into English successfully. Durling's prose translations do not solve the problems of rendering Petrarch's work, but are preferrable to verse trans-lations which go for rhymes and end up with artificial or clunky lines. Rhyming limits the translator too much, I think. In some cases, other translations have been employed.

ONE

୬

THE COURTLY LOVE OF THE TROUBADOURS

Love, it is your praise I sing, for you cause me to love, the most noble – she through whom I'm exalted that even death to me is honourable, she is such a noble excellence. And if I had joy from her, I know I would not die; rather I'd live, finely rewarded.

Guilhelm de Montanhagol (d. late 1250s)[1]

THE COURTLY LOVE ERA

The age of the troubadours is marked by an emphasis on Christianity, on God, and on religious faith. It was the age of monasteries, of saints and theologians, such as St Bernard of Clairvaux with his sermons on the *Song of Songs,* and the teachings of Thomas Aquinas. The Middle Ages abound in saints and martyrs, in all kinds of mystics. The chief religious characters were God, Christ, the Virgin and the Devil. Hell was regarded as a very real place, only inches away from everyday life.

Before the lyrics of the troubadours flowered, the first great wave of poetry was religious – there were hymns, prayers, litanies and intercessions. As Peter Dronke notes in *The Medieval Lyric*:

> the first heights of achievement in our extant repertoire of mediæval European lyric occur in the religious mode, in the second generation after Charlemagne, more than two and a half centuries before secular and vernacular lyrics survive in any abundance. (32)

Passion is central to the mediæval era – both the Passion of Christ, and the passion of lovers. Pain was exalted – evoked in so many crucifixion images (in illuminated books, in sculptures, statues, and paintings), and in so much of the troubadours' poetry. Mysticism blossomed in an extraordinary fashion in the Middle Ages. So many mystics burned for love – Richard of St Victor, Jan van Ruysbroeck, Meister Eckhart, Hildegard of Bingen, St Catherine, Richard Rolle, etc. Female mystics in particular were prominent – such as Hildegard of Bingen, Mechthild of Magdeburg, and Julian of Norwich. Writing was crucial to female mysticism, as Margaret Wade Labarge notes in *Women in Medieval Life*.[2] Despised by the Church and its theologians, women often turned to cults such as Catharism, because there they were 'not only accepted as full members of the sect, they could also join the ranks of the perfect' (M. Labarge, ib., 223).

The eleventh and twelfth centuries saw the growth of religious cults devoted to the Virgin Mary. The Madonna was enshrined in exalted poetry, in the great Cathedrals of Europe, and in the art of the time. The Cathedrals in particular are marvellous: Chartres, Notre Dame, Rouen, Cologne and Canterbury. Later, the Virgin became the Lover of Christ, in art which aimed to create a mediæval version of the spiritual marriage, the *hieros gamos* of occultism.

The Virgin presides over much of mediæval art. Dante Alighieri and Francesco Petrarch both exalted her, and aspects of the Madonna can be seen in Beatrice and Laura. In many ways the Madonna is a mediæval/ European reincarnation of the

Goddesses of old – Isis, Ishtar, Sophia, Diana, etc. The Virgin is still, of course, very much a patriarchal creation, made by men and for men. That is, the Madonna is a masculinist construct, a myth, an archetype, having little or nothing to do with actual women or real women's issues.

The troubadours exalted women, and the later *stil novisti* exalted the Madonna, but things were just as bad for women in the Middle Ages as they always were. Rape was common; women were regarded as property; and marriage was a matter of a materialist exchange.[3] Some theologians had extraordinarily twisted views of women. They hated women, there's no doubt about it, at least according to their writings. Francesco Petrarch too, even though he praised Laura to the skies in his poesie, echoed the dire women-hating polemics of chauvinists such as theologians of the early Christian Church such as Origen, Tertullian, Augustine and St Jerome. Courtly love turns out to be severely patriarchal. At every step it reinforces masculinist views of women.

HERESY: THE UNDERBELLY OF CHRISTIANITY

In the Middle Ages a number of sects, cults and beliefs became prominent. Cults such as Catharism were regarded as heresy by the Christian orthodoxy. But in fact such Gnostic belief systems lie at the foundation of Christianity. Indeed, at one point, Gnosticism threatened to overwhelm Christianity (in the early years). The troubadour poets were deemed heretical, as were the Knights Templar. The Templars annoyed the authorities probably because they were rich, powerful, ascetic and pure in their religious beliefs. In a way, they did everything noble and pure that the people in power wished to do but couldn't (for whatever reason).

The Knights Templar embody much of the metaphysical and ethical notions of the age: the monastic/ ascetic lifestyle, the intensely-held religious beliefs, the fusion of faith and action, the emphasis on ritual, etc.

The Templars were great Arthurian figures. After the Christian mystical texts, and the lyrics of the troubadours, the Arthurian romances were the richest creations of the era in literature. Indeed, courtly love merges with monastic mysticism and Arthurian romance at many points. A revived cult of the feminine principle is a hallmark of mediæval poetry, mysticism and romance. So is secrecy – the Templars, the troubadour poets and the Gnostic sects were all very secretive. The troubadours sang in courts, but the love relationships enshrined in their songs were enacted away from the public's gaze.

At one time, courtly love was thought of as a heresy by some commentators. In fact there is nothing threatening about it – but religionists (the Pope, the King and their regimes) have always moved against detractors and unbelievers.[4]

THE GARDEN OF LOVE

Much of masculinist culture in mediæval times exalted aggression – the Arthurian brotherhoods, the Crusades, the codes of chivalry, gallantry, pageantry and hunting. In the mediæval illuminated manuscripts, in those gorgeous, gilded *Books of Hours, Bibles* and prayer books, the hunting and falconry scenes look so enchanting, so innocent. But the hunts, like the Crusades themselves, must have been gruelling and violent.

One creation of the age is gentler – the garden of love, the *hortus conclusus* (= enclosed garden), typically a rose garden where lovers would meet. The image of the love garden is straight out of Classical, pastoral imagery, out of the verses of Horace and Virgil. In the bucolic scenario of the ancient world, a shepherdess would be seduced by a noble (Thomas Hardy reworked this ballad-like story in his 1891 novel *Tess of the d'Urbervilles*). In courtly love poetry, the enclosed garden functions as a sacred place in which lovers can meet on equal terms. The dream is of Arcadia, a lost Eden.

One deeper meaning of the *hortus conclusus* is that it represents the Virgin Mary. The walled garden is her intact womb, her purity and virginity. The garden becomes an image of the womb of the Goddess. Since earliest times Goddesses have been associated with the Earth, with growth, agriculture, plants, flowers, the seasons and (re-)birth.

The associations of woman = goddess = womb = garden = agriculture = seasons = moon = nature = Earth = birth are deep, widespread and very ancient.[5] The Goddesses of old were called 'Goddesses of Flowers';[6] in Ovid's poetry, she is Flora, 'the Mother of Flowers'. Francesco Petrarch, a number of times in the *Rime Sparse*, relates Laura to a nature or Earth Goddess, and she is a Goddess of Flowers throughout the poem sequence. Further, the sacred space of the enclosed garden is where much of Petrarch's poetry takes place, as with the troubadours.

One enters the walled garden as one enters the holy place of one's beloved. To enter the rose garden is to return to Eden. The garden is the womb, and everything in it flourishes. One enters Heaven: the connections are made in courtly love poetry between the secret chamber of the beloved and the beloved's womb; the garden becomes Heaven or Eden, and a love-meeting in a garden is to regain Paradise (in Arnaut Daniel's lyrics, and in St Bernard's *Song of Songs* sermons, for instance).

I mention the garden of love because it plays such a large part in the poetry of Dante Alighieri, Francesco Petrarch and the troubadours. The rose garden has a further feature that Dante and Petrarch make use of: the symbolism of the rose. The rose is the premier symbolic flower of the West – its counterpart in the

Orient being the lotus of Buddha. The rose is deeply feminine, a symbol of nature in abundance, and also the eroticism of the vulva and womb with its watery petals. The colour, too, is that of the Goddess (there are many other symbolic associations with the rose).

The love garden is an urban version of the Classical, pastoral scene. It is a part of the city, being sited adjacent to the main house in a community. Christopher Hacker writes, in *The History of Gardens*:

> Commonly, the mediæval garden of pleasure, whether knightly or spiritual, will centre around a 'flowery mede', a space of a meadow-grass sprinkled with innumerable flowers, where Adam and Eve, Virgin and Child, knights and ladies will gather together for moments of recreation and delight. (1979, 10)

It sounds dreamily heavenly, because that is precisely what it is, a sacred space where the holy replaces the profane, where sacred time is re-introduced, where acts attain their proper poetic weight. The garden of love is the place most troubadours would like to live in, eternally.

THE UNICORN AND THE VIRGIN

The unicorn in the garden is an enigmatic image of the mediæval garden, so beautifully portrayed in the famous Cluny tapestries in Paris. Only a virgin can tame a unicorn, so the legends say. Symbolically, the unicorn can depict Christ, laying his head in the lap of the Virgin Mother. There are also portrayals of the 'mystic hunt', where the Archangel Gabriel blows a horn (as in *The Allegory of the Annunciation, c.* 1420, German, Erfurt Cathedral).

Psychologically, the unicorn can be seen as wholly erotic – he lays his phallic horn in the lap of the virgin ('lap' is a typical stand-in linguistically for the vulva or womb). Or the unicorn can be the agent of initiation and individuation, an achieved, questing Jungian self.

There are Petrarchan symbolic connections, too, between the unicorn, the Virgin Mary, the Goddess Diana (the huntress or quester) and Chastity (in Francesco Petrarch's *Triumphs*). Only the virgin (Laura or Mary) can tame (satisfy sexually or spiritually) the lusty, earthy, phallic unicorn (the poet, the desirer).

THE VIRGIN WITH A MIRROR

Sometimes the Virgin Mary is depicted alone in the enclosed garden, holding a mirror. The symbolism of the mirror is connected to the purity of the Madonna (the 'mirror without blemish'). In *La Roman de la Dame à la Lycorne et du Biau Chevalier au Lyon*, the knight likens his beloved to a 'mirror… clear, shining, unsullied'.[7]

One deeper meaning of the mirror is that, as Virginia Woolf said, women are mirrors, who reflect the acts of men. Without their mirrors, men feel so alone. They need mirrors (women, praise, acknowledgement, the media) to make their actions meaningful and mythic. Throughout the poetry of the troubadours, the *stil novisti*, Dante Alighieri and Francesco Petrarch, women act as mirrors, reflecting the poet's emotions, hopes, ideas and desires. The mirror acts too as an image of the soul, and the image the poet sees reflected there is also his *anima*, his soul-image, his beloved.

Sometimes the Virgin Mary is depicted amongst a company of virgins, the *virgin inter virgines* image. Such a solidarity of women is very strong, able to withstand male advances and projections. Paintings of the Virgin among virgins exclude men (except perhaps a gardener, as in Gerard David's panel in the National Gallery, London).

In the grass one finds the flowers associated with the Madonna: the rose ('love's own flower'),[8] the iris, the lily, the violet, and the carnation. The colours of mediæval gardens are white and red, roses and lilies. These colours also dominate William Shakespeare's *Sonnets*. The colours are those of life itself, of alchemy, the black-white-red noted by Georg Groddeck among others.[9] The red is the colour of passion, anger, sex (menstrual) blood; it is the colour of life in ascension, of things blooming at their height. It is the colour Stone Age people used to paint bones in their barrows and tombs.

Black is the colour of death, the unknown, night, secrecy, evil, mourning, etc. But it's also the colour of the Black Goddess, the supersensual deity who stands behind the White Goddess (in the mythopœia of Robert Graves).[10] Black is then a very positive colour, signifying occultism, the paranormal, the sixth sense. White meanwhile is the colour of purity, virginity, Heaven and the known world.

The symbolism of colours, flowers, gardens, mirrors, eyes, gestures, landscapes and animals is important in gaining a deeper understanding of courtly love poetry. Dante and Petrarch trade in mediæval symbolism continually. Their poesies are full of images of roses, beasts (from the mediæval bestiaries), symbolic colours, particular places and hieratic gestures. One of the most sumptuous and magical of all depictions of the Virgin Mary is Stefan Lochner's *Madonna In the Rose Garden* (*c*. 1440, Wallraf-Richhartz Museum, Cologne). Lochner's sweet image contains strawberries, clover, violets, roses and daises.[11]

The most consistently mesmerizing images of the Madonna in an enclosed garden are those of the Early Netherlandish school – Jan van Eyck, Bernard Van Orley, Rogier Van Der Weyden, Hans Memling and Deiric Bouts. In their luminous, exquisitely detailed pictures, the Virgin Mary is exalted in a way wholly in tune with that of the troubadours, Dante and Petrarch. The Early Flemish Madonnas, like those of the Italian Renaissance painters such as Andrea del Sarto, Fra Filippo Lippi and Leonardo da Vinci, are clearly based on real women. In Sarto's case, his wife Lucrezia modelled for many *Virgin* pictures, echoing that fusion of mortal women and the immortal Madonna which we find in the poetry of Dante and Petrarch.

In the visual arts of the Middle Ages, we see the colourful, religious manifestations of the faces, landscapes and events of courtly love poetry. The illuminations, miniatures, stained glasses and Cathedrals take us instantly into the mediæval world. We can look past the idealized vistas and faces and see the frailty and flaws of the humanity beyond. The awkward gestures, the often ugly, misshapen faces, the crudely-drawn architecture, the child-like landscapes populated by dragons, basilisks, lions, deer and peacocks, all these things contribute towards our picture of the mediæval world, which is the world of the troubadours, of Dante, Cavalcanti and Petrarch.

TWO

֍

THE RELIGION OF LOVE

tan ai al cor d'anor,
de joi e de doussor,
per que.l gels me sembla flore
e la neus verdursa.
(I have in my heart so much joy and sweetness from love that the ice
appears to me as blossom and the snow as greenery).

Bernard de Ventadour[1]

THE EROTICISM OF THE LOOK

The look, the gaze, is all important in courtly love poetry, and in
all love poetry. The troubadours constantly emphasized the eyes,
seeing the beloved (usually from afar – the *amor lonh*). The visual
sense is the primary sense in troubadour poetry. As the French
psychologist Jacques Lacan said, the look is erotic; it is central to
eroticism and love. The look lies at the heart of love poetry, and of
much of Western culture (the voyeur and the look in cinema, for
instance, or the (usually masculine) gaze in painting and porno-
graphy, which looks at the obscure object of desire, the (female)
beloved.)

The mechanism of the Lacanian look is explained lucidly by Jack Zipes in one of his books on fairy tales:

> For him [Lacan], seeing is desire, and the eye functions as a kind of phallus. However, the eye cannot clearly see its object of desire, and in the case of male desire, the female object of desire is an illusion created by the male unconscious.
>
>   Or, in other words, the male desire for woman expressed in the gaze is auto-erotic and involves the male's desire to have his own identity reconfirmed in a mirror image.[2]

Here we see how the mirror and the unicorn fits in, and how most of (male) love poetry does precisely this: it pivots around an illusion, a projection, which ultimately is self-reflexive. The (masculine) exaltation of the love object (the woman) finally is an exaltation of the poet himself. This is clear when we look at the lyrics of Dante Alighieri or Francesco Petrarch. William Shakespeare in the *Sonnets* spoke of the eye '[g]ilding the object whereupon it gazeth' (sonnet 20, line 6).

The look, then, is an assertion of masculine sexuality and power within the context of patriarchal culture. Pornography revolves, æsthetically, around the masculine look, and pornography is love poetry taken to extremes. The links between the eye and the phallus were fully exploited in Georges Bataille's *The Story of the Eye*, which is regarded in *avant garde* circles as a work of high class pornography, or intellectual erotica. Bataille placed eyes in vulvas, mouths and anuses, thereby taking the Sadeian ethic of the pornographic look to its logical conclusion. In Bataille's fiction we see the metaphysics of courtly love portrayed in a violent, modern manner. But the values and attitudes are still those of courtly love. Modern pornography is courtly love without the gentleness, but it is still 'love from afar', *amor lonh,* the eroticism of the voyeur. In courtly love as in pornography, men gaze at women who are manipulated into erotic poses.[3]

In "Lacan, Literature and the Look", Larysa Nykyta writes:

> the sexual triumph of the male passes through the eye, through the

contemplation of the woman. Seeing the women ensures the satisfaction of wanting to be seen, of having one's desire recognized, and thus comes back to the original aim of the scopic drive. Woman is repressed as subject and desired as object in order to efface the gaze of the Other, the gaze that would destroy the illusion of reciprocity and oneness that the process of seeing usually supports. The female object does not look, does not have its own point of view; rather it is erected as an image of the phallus sustaining male desire.[4]

This is a good, accurate reading of love poetry, of the mechanisms that operate throughout the poetry of Francesco Petrarch and Dante Alighieri, and the troubadours. The post-Lacanian methodology helps to explain the emotional dynamic of much of love poetry. In Jungian psychology we hear of the *anima*, the feminine image in the male: certainly, much of (male) love poetry concerns the projection of unconscious desires embodied in a female figure (who became, in the most idealized version, the Virgin Mary). But post-Lacanian theory helps to describe the operation and meaning of the deep communication (or lack of it) between the poet/ artist and the woman/ beloved. Cultural theory exposes the psychological pressure of literature; it demonstrates how much pressure is placed upon the obscure object of desire by the poet. Writing itself can become in masculine hands a form of repression: women are silenced by men, denied the chance to speak. There were female troubadours, in amongst the four hundred male troubadours, but they are rarely acknowledged by critics. As the French feminist Xavière Gauthier wrote in "Why Witches?":

> The frightful masculine fashion of speaking always surprises me. Speaking in order to be right – how ridiculous! In fact, to put someone else in the wrong. Speaking to nail the listener's trap shut. Speaking to put her in her place: man's language, man's rod.[5]

We've all met a few people who speak like this, who speak in order to silence the listener. The connections between writing and seeing, between literary culture and visual culture, and between the male artist and the female object, have always been at the heart of art. In courtly love poetry, these links are made explicit, and form the foundation of the 'religion of love'.

As Julia Kristeva says in *Revolution in Poetic Language*, 'isn't art the fetish *par excellence*, one that badly camouflages its archeology?' (115) The art object is indeed the erotic object *par excellence* in art. It is the phallus endlessly caressed by the eyes, in Lacanian, scopic, scopophillic, voyeuristic pleasure.

On one level, artistic creation counters Lacanian lack and Kristevan absence: the act of writing staves off emptiness and loneliness by filling up the psychic space. As Julia Kristeva wrote in "Freud and Love: Treatment and Its Discontents":

> If narcissism is a defence against the emptiness of separation, then the whole contrivance of imagery, representations, identifications and projections that accompany it on the way towards strengthening the Ego and the Subject is a means of exorcising that emptiness. (*Tales of Love*, 42)

In her psychoanalyst mode, Julia Kristeva reckons that art is born out of the pain of loss. She asserts:

> the creative act is released by an experience of depression without which we could not call into question the stability of meaning or the banality of expression. A writer must at one time or another have been in a situation of loss – of ties, of meaning – in order to write.[6]

THE EYES OF LOVE

> A subtle spirit wounds through the eyes which causes a spirit to arise in the soul from which is born a spirit of love such as that all other spirits are made gentle through it.

> Guido Cavalcanti, "Per gli occhi"[7]

Love begins with sight, and pierces to the heart and the soul via the eyes. The moment when love enters the eyes and heart fuses sex and death, which the troubadours glossed as love and pain. Since before the age of Sappho, sex and death have been fused in art. Love-pain is the subject matter of the troubadours and of the love poet of all ages.

In *La Roman de la Rose,* a famous and anonymous mediæval text (*c.* 1230-1280), the narrator is pierced by love's arrow (a literal, physical arrow) – it is an erotic moment, and also violent (an arrow piercing the body is no gentle occurrence):

> Love selected another arrow, worked in gold. It was the second arrow and its name was Simplicity. It has caused many a man and woman all over the world to fall in love.[8]

This is the way the poet-characters in the poetry of Dante Alighieri and Francesco Petrarch fall in love: at first sight, and violently. In *The Romance of the Rose* we also hear of the dreamer Narcissus, who stares at his reflection in a pool. The image precisely describes the self-absorption of the poet in love, and the narcissistic state of being in love. Like Lancelot in Chrétien de Troyes' romance, the lover daydreams of his beloved. It is in this love-stupor that the poet writes her/ his poetry.

No poet writes so obsessively about the beloved's eyes as Francesco Petrarch does, except perhaps Bill Shakespeare. Eyes and vision are prime symbols and motifs in Shakespeare's *Sonnets*. In sonnet 75 we read:

Sometime all full with feasting on your sight,
And by and by clean starved for a look... (9-10)

The love poet yearns for just one look from the beloved. A look is often enough. In Dante Alighieri's *Vita Nuova* the poet dwells on Beatrice's eyes to the exclusion of nearly everything else. In part XX, Dante writes that a

worthy lady's beauty next is viewed
with pleasure by the eyes (VN, 39)

In all love poetry seeing is pleasurable, and what the courtly love poet wishes to see is not the Freudian primal scene but great beauty. Beauty is the goal of the troubadours' vision quest.

Francesco Petrarch's poesie eulogized Laura de Sade's eyes many times in the *Canzoniere*. Early on in the sequence, in sonnet 3, Petrarch describes how love found its way into his heart through his eyes and adds that his eyes 'are now the portal and passageway of tears' (*Petrarch's Lyric Poems*, 38). Already, Petrarch moves into the future, into his solitude, and looks back on the first time he fell in love with Laura. Even at this early stage of the *Rime Sparse* he is speaking nostalgically, weighing up the experience in retrospect.

Francesco Petrarch calls Laura's eyes the sun's rays (9), fated stars (17), Heaven's light shines from them (72), they are 'lovely angelic sparks' (72.37), delicious (135), and so on. He is transfixed by her eyes; Laura's eyes have the powers of a god: 'with her glance she steals' (23.72); again, in *canzone* 37, the poet complains of 'that lovely clear gaze' where the rays of love 'are so hot that they kill me before my time' (37.83-85); the poet is so and was so mesmerized by Laura's eyes that they haunt him for years – their power grows:

Fuggir vorrei, ma gli amorosi rai
che di et notte ne la mente stanno
risplendon si ch' al quintodecimo anno
m'abbaglian piu che 'l primo giorno assai...

(I wish I could flee, but those love-inspiring rays, which are in my mind night and day, shine so that at the fifteenth year they dazzle me much more than on the first day) (107.5-8)

Clearly Laura possessed extraordinary eyes, or Francesco Petrarch thought she did, or the dazzlement is purely poetic. Perhaps Laura had what Lawrence Durrell called 'the Taoist look',[9] which is a glance of intensity, complicity and self-deprecation. A *knowing* look, above all one which is aware of a cosmic dimension to life as much as a human one. Men know the power of the look. When women look at men in poems the look is controlled, shaped, æstheticized. The beloved's eyes become a mirror in which the poet sees his desire reflected. The more intense, refined and beautiful and worthy the desire, the more intense, refined, beautiful and worthy is the reflection.

THE CODES OF COURTLY LOVE

The codes of courtly love pivot around the poet's relationship with the beloved. The relationship is heterosexual and employs traditional gender roles. The woman is exalted in feudal terms, as a Lord, but the real Lord is not God but Love. Courtly *amor* lies at the heart of courtly love. The lady is loved from afar (*fin amor lonh*); the relation is that of a knight and a lord; the relation replaces the lord with the lady (much as women sometimes ran courts while men went away to fight their 'noble' Crusades); the poet sings to please the lady; the poet expects nothing in return; the poet often courts a lady for years.

The codes of courtly love are also those of mediæval gallantry and chivalry, where knights swear oaths of allegiance and fealty to a lord, and become his vassals. The language of chivalry, falconry, feasting, song and courtly life finds its way into the troubadours' works; similarly, the troubadours use much religious language and imagery.

For critics such as C.S. Lewis (in *The Allegory of Love*), courtly love sprang from nowhere, but other commentators have recognized that passionate and individual love existed in Classical Greece, indeed, probably, at all times of human history. It is not love that is new with the troubadours, but a way of writing about love. The art of love and how it is portrayed is what is new in courtly love culture. As Robert Hollander noted in *Boccaccio's Two Venuses*, the religion of love was 'a literary tradition' (1977, 4). It was an artistic as much as a moral movement; it was much concerned with artifice; and it only exists now in poetry.

Commentators seem to look back at the courtly love era with affection, as if it was a golden age, an age of innocence and paradise. In much the same way, Francesco Petrarch looked back from his era to the Classical Age, which he preferred in many ways. In his *Letter To Posterity,* Petrarch wrote: 'I devoted myself to the study of antiquity, for I always disliked our own age'.[10] In his *De vita solitaria,* he said: 'I am alive now yet I would rather have been born at some other time'[11] (I often feel that way myself).

The codes of courtly love exalt honour, dignity, discipline, pride, loyalty, perseverance, restraint, passion and asceticism. The lover is expected to suffer anything for his beloved. It all sounds wonderful, but the actuality must have been very different. The troubadours' lyrics were produced for a large, court audience. Troubadours sang their own material, or had people to sing for them – by the *jongleur* or minstrel (the *joglar* in Provençal). Music was crucial to the troubadours' songs: we lose the vocal and musical nature of the troubadours' works now, when we read them, silently, in books.

In one sense, then, courtly love poetry was mass entertainment, produced for ever more sophisticated and discerning consumers. The private side of it – how it worked between real people in difficult situations (i.e., ordinary life) – is not known so clearly. There is no doubt, though, that courtly love poetry was created from actual love experiences. The intensity of the lyrics may not be strictly autobiographical, but it certainly stems from a deep understanding of human relationships.

LOVE AND SEX

> Del cors li fos, non de l'arma,
> e cossentis m'a celat dinz sa cambra!
> (Would that I might be hers with my body, not with my soul, and that she might admit me in secret to her room!)
>
> Arnaut Daniel[12]

The troubadours write about sex a great deal: the desire for it, the agony of it, the memory of it. Sex, usually the lack of it, is a major theme in *amour courtois*. Reduced to its bare essentials, *courtoisie* concerns men lusting after the 'quene of cortesye', the luscious 'Donna Gentile'. As Arnaut Daniel says, forget my soul, take my body! Francesco Petrarch called Daniel the 'gran mæstro d'amor' (quoted in A. Press, 174), and he is one of the most highly regarded of all troubadours (Dante Alighieri greatly admired him).

Arnaut Daniel's art merges sexuality and spirituality freely. Daniel combined human and divine love long before Dante Alighieri and Francesco Petrarch (in his poem quoted above, "Lo ferm voler").

In the Louvre Museum in Paris there is a plate which depicts a group of men kneeling in a garden of love. The Goddess Venus, nude, floats above them. Lines are drawn between the men's eyes and Venus's vulva. Each man is shown staring straight at the sex of the Goddess.

Sex is always present in courtly love poetry, even when the poet studiously skirts the subject. The relationship itself, between the poet/ knight/ lover and the beloved/ lady, is sexual. The act of looking is sexual, the look of the lady is sexual, and the act of writing is erotic.

Venus opposes the Virgin Mary symbolically in mediæval culture: Venus is of the pagan/ ancient world, while the Madonna is of the Christian/ mediæval era. Venus/ Aphrodite is a holy whore, while Mary/ Sophia is a sacred virgin, a spotless mother. The Goddess of the troubadours, and of Dante Alighieri, Francesco Petrarch and the *stil novisti*, seems to be the Blessed Virgin Mary, the Holy Mother of God. But Venus/ Aphrodite is a strong presence underneath the surface sheen of respectability and establishment *mœurs*.

Ambivalence is a hallmark of courtly love and love poetry. The poets veer between fear and desire, despair and hope, asceticism (monastic chastity) and sexual pleasure. The Christian fathers and theologians similarly outline opposing forms of love. There was the *caritas* and the *cupiditas* of St Augustine;[13] Thomas Aquinas spoke of the importance of 'Charity',[14] while St Bernard described love in very sensual terms.[15]

All of these forms of mediæval (Christian) love (*eros, agape, amor naturalis, amos rationalis, caritas, cupiditas*, etc), are essentially ways of explaining or symbolizing the eternal duality of sacred and profane, divine and human, spiritual and sexual, heavenly and earthly, holy and everyday.

The conflict between the sacred and the profane is an old one, whether in the realm of religion, art, love or life. When the guardians of Christianity (St Paul, St Augustine, Tertullian, Origen, etc) focussed on love, they got into terrible confusions. *Deus est caritas*: God is Love, they said, but human love has always had a deep sexual component. Christianity tries, therefore, to desexualize love (for any number of reasons. Erotic love is threatening – it disrupts the moral equilibrium. Perhaps this was one reason why the creators of Christian ethics struggled to smother it.)

A central tenet of magic and occultism is 'as above, so below.' This is not so in Christianity. There is no sex in Heaven. The extraordinarily energetic hatred of sexuality in Christianity is perplexing. Perhaps this denial of the body stems partly from the exhortations of the most influential Christian thinker, St Paul. His writings, which too often come across as psychotic ravings, unfortunately became doctrine and dogma in Christianity. A more sympathetic interpreter of Christ's teachings might have changed the growth of Christianity, and the history of the world. It didn't help things either by having later theologians such as Tertullian call women 'the gateway to hell'. Hell is slang for the female sex – it occurs in Giovanni Boccaccio's *Decameron*, and in William Shakespeare's *Sonnets* (119.2, 129.14, 144.2) and *King Lear* (IV. vi, 127-8).[16] Christianity is continually ambivalent with regard to women and sex. It never knows quite how to deal with them.

Many mystics – and the Catholic ones especially – speak of mystical ecstasy as sensual, and love becomes the model, metaphor and actuality of God's love. The raptures of the Christian mystics are circumscribed in sexual language (think of St Teresa, St Catherine, St Bernard, Jan van Ruysbroeck, and St John of the Cross). Mysticism uses the language of love, just as the love poets used the language of mysticism to describe their ecstasies.

The object of the religious rapture is God; the object of sexual bliss is the beloved human, but the ecstasies are very similar. The Christian establishment is terrified when sex is mixed with religion, but at the same time it is fascinated, and some of the greatest Christian theologians have written of the union with God in highly erotic terms (St Bernard and Jan van Ruysbroeck, for instance). Mystics such as Richard Rolle and St Teresa talk about being pierced with Love's arrow, about burning feverishly with love.

This erotic prose from the mediæval mystics is precisely mirrored in the lyrics of the troubadours. Images of burning, fires and heat abound in *amour courtois*, and in all love poetry. The fire of love consumes mystics and poets alike. But while mystics die like martyrs in a Joan of Arc conflagration, lovers and poets burn up in the domestic bed.

Richard of St Victor is typical among (mediæval) mystics, when he wrote:

> desiderio ardet, fervet affectu, æsthet, anhelat, profonde ingemscens et longa suspira trahens
> (the lover burns with love-longing, inflamed by his passion. He is all aglow, breathless, moaning deeply and sighing long)[17]

The troubadours write in the same sensual, sighing, emotional fashion: Arnaut Daniel wrote: 'my heart burns, but nothing outside of me burns, since it burns within'.[18] As with mysticism, courtly love exalts suffering. The more terrible the pain, the more exalted the love (when it finally arrives). As Perdigon wrote: 'Blessed be the pains, the sorrows and the cares which I have long suffered because of love.'[19]

Both mysticism and love poetry have a strong sadomasochistic tendency. The troubadours, as with Dante Alighieri and Francesco Petrarch, loved to wallow in love, in their emotions, hopes and despairs. Love poets of all kinds make myths out of their experiences: they mythicize, romanticize and eulogize their love.

This is nothing new. Hundreds of years before the poets of *fin amor*, Sappho had written:

> It [love] brings us pain
> and weaves myths.[20]

This short fragment has the compressed beauty and truth of a Japanese *haiku* poem. The troubadours made mythologies out of love's many pains. The largest literary structure created from/ by/ to/ for love in literature is probably Francesco Petrarch's *Canzoniere*. Sex is not the driving force behind Petrarch's poetic monument, as it is (partly) in William Shakespeare's *Sonnets*.

Rather, Petrarch desires to make contact with the beloved; he also wants fame, poetic immortality, and recognition. Petrarch holds his dignified head above carnal pleasures, in the main. The troubadours were more direct: Beatrice, Countess of Die, wrote:

> Ben volvia mon cavallier
> tener un ser en mos'bratz nut.
> (How I'd long to hold him pressed
> naked in my arms one night)[21]

One of the earliest troubadours, Guilhelm IX of Aquitaine (d. 1127), put his sexual desires even plainer: 'May God let me still live long enough to have my hands beneath her cloak.'[22] Such bald statements remind us how much sex there is in love (poetry), and the value of a caress cannot be under-estimated.

DESIRE

Desire powers love poetry; it is the primary emotion, the driving force, the energy which thrusts the lover forward on the quest for the beloved. In love poetry, the journey is everything. Love poetry pivots around unsatisfied desire. If desire is fulfilled, it loses its potency. Hence all love poets cultivate desire. Without desire, they know that nothing much will happen. Desire makes everything interesting, rich, deep, passionate.

Desire kills, though. 'Desire is death', as Will Shakespeare put it (sonnet 147.8), while Bernard de Ventadour said, 'I detest my desire'.[23] The 'hermeneutics of desire' (Michel Foucault's phrase in *The Use of Pleasure*, 5) in troubadour poetry is deeply erotic: and death is continually mixed in with sex, so that the two exist alongside each other. As the wonderfully acerbic French feminist Hélène Cixous put it in her extraordinary 1975 essay

"The Laugh of the Medusa":

> Men say that there are two unrepresentable things: death and the feminine sex. That's because they need femininity to be associated with death; it's the jitters that give them a hard-on! for themselves! They need to be afraid of us.[24]

Desire is an essential element in many images of women – in the Madonna, for instance, or in the sacred prostitutes of Ancient Greece, or in the artist's model, her limbs arranged for the delight of patrons.

Courtly love poetry overflows with intense yearning. Yearning, desire, longing, wanting, wishing, lusting – these are the emotions of *amour courtois*. As Bayazid of Bistan (d. 874) put it: 'Desire is the capital of the lover's kingdom.'[25] Desire causes fevers in love poets of all ages, from Sappho through William Shakespeare to Constantin Cavafy and beyond.

The desire is for joy (*jois*) which only the beloved lady can bestow upon the eager lover. The power relation expressed in the lyrics is of a meek soul kneeling before the Lord and begging for mercy; the knight kneeling before the lady and asking for *merci*. The lady, as in John Keats' courtly poem, is a *belle dame sans merci*, a *femme fatale*.

The key words in courtly love poetry are *amor, jois, cors, volers, saber, midons*. Joy means a special kind of bliss, at once human and mystical. In the poetry the emphasis is on love before sex, that is, on pure, sweet, true love rather than raw, harsh, quick sex. As Francois Ferguson put it in *Dante*: 'this earliest European love poetry dwells... upon the iridescent colours of the passion itself before the biological mechanisms take over.' (1966, 12) In *The Heresy of Courtly Love*, A.J. Denomy wrote: 'the three basic elements of the conception of love as desire, the ennobling force of love, and the cult of the beloved... make Courtly Love to be Courtly Love'.

Desire ennobles the lover – this is a key theme in *amour courtois*. Simply by loving one would be elevated, or rather, by loving properly. Despite the emphasis on the noble nature of love, lust kept recurring in courtly love poetry. In an anonymous Spanish *kharja*, a colloquial Arabic/ Spanish love song (in 'Mozarabic', *c.* 1000-1150), a woman sings to her lover:

> Tan t'an aray, ilia con
>   al-sarti
> an tasma' halhali ma'
> qurti!
> (I'll give you such love! – but only if you'll bend my anklets right over to my earrings)[26]

Such humorous (and vivid) outbursts cut through the delicate structure of noble love which the troubadours so carefully built. Yet such base desires lie beneath the courtly veneer of the troubadours' poetry. As with Ovid, Sappho, Catullus and many of the Ancient Greek epigrammatists, the troubadours were openly erotic in their *cansos*. While an orgasmic union with the beloved was the Holy Grail of many poems, desire itself, the journey towards the goal, was often enough.

Plato, a major influence on courtly love, as on the whole of Western culture, said in his *Symposium*:

> Each of us when separated is always looking for his other half; such a nature is prone to love and ready to return love. And when he finds his other half, the pair are lost in an amazement of love and friendship and intimacy... For the entire yearning which each of them has toward the other does not appear to be the desire of intercourse, but of something else which the soul cannot tell and of which she has only a dark and doubtful presentiment.[27]

Plato's notion is that of the Gnostic *syzygy*, where two souls are joined together like two yokes in an egg. This Gnostic concept, arising out of Neoplatonism, is the basis of romantic love: the idea of an ideal that there is one's 'other half' out there somewhere, that one is not complete until one is joined to one's partner.

This idea lies behind marriage, behind the Harlequin or Mills and Boon romance in fiction, and the fairy tale which ends with a wedding where everyone lives 'happily ever after'. It is a wish, a utopian desire, and also a lie, of course, the Noble Lie of Platonism; but it forms the foundation of Western love.

On the surface *fin amor* was a cultivated game, a sport, an elegant battle fought in feudalist ways. But underneath is the dream of the Neoplatonic union, the *hieros gamos* (spiritual marriage) of occultism, the *unio mystica* of religion. Religious thinkers such as Lanfranc, St Anselm, Peter Abelard, Peter Damion, Jan van Ruysbroeck and Meister Eckhart all spoke of this ideal of a spiritual union. It is a dream, though, just as the unicorn, the famous animal of the *Physiologus* and the bestiaries, is a dream, albeit a very popular one.[28]

Desire kills, but it must be kept alive and thriving if love and poetry are to flourish. Desire must be kept unfulfilled, as A.J. Denomy says in *Medieval Studies:*

> Love must remain a desire in order that the end may be fulfilled. Once consummated, desire weakens and consequently growth in virtue and worth lessens. (176)

This is a typical masculine view of love and desire. But it is true that the fairy tale ends with the wedding of the prince and princess, and the Mills and Boon or Harlequin romance novel finishes with the consummation of the marriage. In mysticism there is nothing to follow the union with God, except perhaps more of the same. Mystical union is regarded as an end in itself, and any means to this end is deemed justified.

Christianity, and therefore courtly love, emphasizes sin and vice. The cycle is from sin to confession to punishment. In Christian religion, every action has to be justified and observed. The eyes of God are everywhere, always looking. Even in marriage, desire is seen as a sin by the more ascetic theologians.

There is always, then, punishment for lovers. Lovers subvert the moral order with the intensity of their passion, and retribution, whether divine or human, is often forthcoming. Punishment for loving is a common theme in Elizabethan tragedy (such as *'Tis Pity She's a Whore* and *Romeo and Juliet*), and in Romantic fictions such as *Wuthering Heights*.

Christianity preaches its idea of love endlessly, at every point in its history. There are only a few kinds of love that are condoned (brotherly love, parental love, love of God and compassion). The myriad forms of sexuality in relationships are ignored or suppressed by the Christian religion.

So it is easy to see how courtly love could be regarded as a heresy at the time, by certain moral authorities, when in fact it is an everyday type of love. As Maurice Valency, one of the finest commentators on mediæval love poetry, wrote in his excellent book *In Praise of Love: An Introduction to the Love-Poetry of the Renaissance*: '[t]he eleventh century, then, did not invent the romantic passion, but it made it fashionable.' (35)

LOVE AS A RELIGION

I do not want to enter into the complex and controversial arguments of the origins of courtly love in Moorish, Arabic and Greek cultures, but there are many parallels to be drawn between the culture of the troubadours and that of the Islamic poets in the Islamic romance of *Wis and Ranin*, for instance, by the Persian poet Gorgani (11th century).

Islamic poetry is extraordinarily passionate and beautiful, and is more intense even than Dante Alighieri, Francesco Petrarch or the troubadours. One only has to mention the names of the Sufi poets arid mystics and recall their poetry to realize the immensity of their achievement: Jalal al-Din Rumi, Mansur al-Hallaj, Farid al-Din Attar, Rabia al-Adawiya, Nur al-Din Abd al-Rahman Jami, and Abu Hamid Muhammad ibn Muhammad al-Ghazzali. Rumi is perhaps the greatest mystical poet of all, greater even than

Dante, St John of the Cross, William Blake or Matsuo Basho.

The Islamic religion of love is truly astonishing: the fierceness and intensity of it overwhelms other mystical poets and other kinds of mystical poetry. Only occasionally do the troubadours reach near the heights of the mediæval Arabic poets. It is worth noting too, while on the subject of Islamic culture, that the science, art and learning of Arabia far surpassed that of mediæval Europe.

There are many symbolic, mythic, psychological and social connections to be made between many mediæval cults, arts and belief systems: between the chivalrous codes espoused in Geoffrey of Monmouth's *Historia Regum Britanniæ* and Chrétien de Troyes' *Lancelot*; between the Gnosticism of the cults of Mary Magdalene, the Black Virgin, the Templars, the Albigensians, and the Manichean beliefs latent in some of the troubadours; between the lovers in the versions of *Tristan and Isolde* and the lovers in *La Roman de la Rose*, and so on.

The key texts and authors of the era – Robert Wace, Chrétien de Troyes, *Sir Gawain and the Green Knight*, Andreas Capellanus' *The Art of Courtly Love*, Gottfried von Strassburg, *The Romance of the Rose* and the versions of the *Tristan and Isolde* romance – combine to form a picture of the world, a sociology of morals and manners, a mythology of love, and a religious viewpoint which if it does not form a unity, at least creates a powerful psycho-social fabric.

Perhaps commentators look back fondly to the mediæval world because there was some kind of social and religious unity – a unity which is entirely lacking today (in 21st century societies in the Western world).

In the Middle Ages, things seemed to be simpler: there was God, Hell, Heaven, Cathedrals, castles, lords, ladies, farmers and peasants. Everything seemed to fit, everything seemed to have its place. But clearly this is an idealized, conservative view of the past. In actuality it must have been as harsh, violent, confused, unjust, ignoble, racist, sexist, and as difficult as any other era.

Andreas Capellanus's treatise on love said: 'Every act ends in the thought of the beloved' (1961, 185). This tenet could be applied to any school of love poetry. Certainly it is a central dictum of Islam, which states that 'there is no God but Allah'. The thought of the Islamic mystic must always be on Allah. As Dhu'l-Nun said: 'in Thee my whole ambition lies'.[29]

The Islamic mystic aches to be dissolved in Allah – this is a total obliteration, not the blasphemous 'union' with God which Catholic mystics speak of. Love is not God, either, as it is in Christianity. But love is always stressed:

> the lover joys to dwell
> in love with Love

Says Yahya b. Mu'adh.[30] The central doctrine of Sufism is 'oneness of being',[31] whereas Christian mysticism is never so ruthless: there is no utter obliteration in Christianity – something of the self, the precious Occidental ego, always remains. The Western mystic, like the Western lover and poet, clings onto that last part of themselves.

While not as severe and intense as Islam, courtly love was nevertheless a religion, 'a religion in the full sense of the word', as Denis de Rougemont put it in *L'Amour et L'Occident* (130). As Stendhal notes, in his wonderful study of love, *De l'Amour*, the concept of love in twelfth century Provence, with its delicate, formalized gestures and refined feelings, was a strange and special occurrence (165f). The progress in courtly love, as in St Bernard's sermons, was 'from carnal to spiritual love'.[32]

In Christianity, God comes first and from Him love flows. In courtly love, love flows from Love – 'Love' is and is not the monolithic God of Western religion. Rather, Love is a mysterious third element, a third power, (Venus, Cupid), perhaps the relationship itself, or perhaps the 'Magickal Child' of occultism, the præternatural bond between people deeply in love (the 'Magickal Child' is a way of symbolizing the love relationship itself: there is a flesh-and-blood child, of course, in love unions and marriages, but there is also love itself, the love created between two people. In occultism, and specifically in alchemy, that is sometimes defined as a third element: two lovers plus love, or the 'Magickal Child').

The troubadours, like all love poets, deified love. When love becomes Love with a capital 'L' (or Eros, Cupid, Amor, etc), it assumes the power of a deity. It can act upon and affect the lovers. In turn, the lovers create a mythology of love. Love then has its own rituals, its own jargon or code-words, its initiation rites (the first sight of the beloved perhaps), and its own High Mass (a kiss, or love-making). Like religion, love has its saints and martyrs, its gods and goddesses, its myths, tales, rites and gestures. The lovers themselves are central to mediæval fictions: Tristan and Isolde, Lancelot and Guinevere, Abelard and Héloise, and later, Dante and Beatrice, and Petrarch and Laura.

Magicians and witches perform the 'five-fold kiss', and the troubadours similarly ritualized looks, gestures, postures and states of mind. The rituals of love enable the poet to get closer to *jois*, joy, the bliss experience of courtly love. Then, in the ecstasy of love, the world becomes transformed.

Troubadours often speak of the amazing powers of love to transform the world. Suddenly, in the middle of Winter, everything is green and blossoming; though it's dark, the sun shines; it is flowery May in snowy Winter; grey turns to rainbows. Many people have spoken of this power of transformation that love is capable of: the troubadour poets set about cultivating it in finely-crafted verses.

EXAMPLES OF TROUBADOUR POETRY

Troubadour poetry is very sensual; it exalts the self, the poet and her/ his subjectivity; there is eternal tension, with no closure; personal details are expunged; the space of the poem, the magic circle it casts about itself, as Robert Graves put it, is timeless; involving a sense of great distance (psychic, social and geographical) between the poet and her/ his beloved; the poet addresses the lady, Love, other poets, and the song itself. Troubadour poets analyze themselves continually, and the art of poetry. Love and art are entwined.

A good, true, pure love demands a good, true, pure poem. The beautiful in life (the beloved) must be matched by the beautiful in art (the poem).

Troubadours such as Giraut de Borneil, Arnaut Daniel and Pierre d'Alvernhe spoke of the unity of love and art in this way.

The centrepiece of troubadour poetry is the *chanson d'amour* or *canso* – the love song. The troubadour poets took pride in their creations, in the intricate rime schemes and forms. The *canso* had to be as refined and as highly finished as possible. Arnaut Daniel speaks of this in a famous poem, of which this is the first stanza:

> En cest sonet coind'e leri
> Faue motz, e capuig e doli,
> Que serant verai e cert
> Qan n'aurai passat la lima;
> Q'Amors marves plan 'e daura
> Nfin chantar, que de liei mou
> Qui pretz manten e governa.
> (In this little song, pretty and gay,
> I compose words, plane and
> polish them,
> so that they will be true and certain when I have
> passed the file over them.
> For Love immediately smooths and gilds my
> singing, which originates from her who possesses and controls
> deserving.)[33]

Poets such as Giraut de Borneil and Arnaut Daniel speak of polishing, fashioning and shaping their poems, as if the set of words and sounds were some gorgeous altarpiece carved from a beautiful chunk of oak or holly and gilded and painted with the meticulous care and dedication of a craftsperson. This attention to form is only one aspect of courtly love poetry that makes it so fresh and modern.

Like Francesco Petrarch, Giraut de Borneil is a poet's poet – highly self-conscious, and very much concerned with the art and theory of poetry.

Giraut de Borneil wrote *vers, cansos, sirventes, albas, tensos* and *pastorelas* – a wide variety of genres.[34] Giraut is one of the handful of first rate troubadours – among them Bernard de Ventadour, Macabru, Arnaut Daniel, Raimbaut d'Aurenga and Pierre d'Alvernhe.

Bernard de Ventadour is typical among troubadours; his verse is highly emotional, yet always finely controlled:

> when she stole herself from me
> she left me nothing except desire
> and a heart filled with longing.[35]

Poets such as Jaufre Rudel were aware of the paradoxes and difficulties of desire:

> I am so full of desire for this love
> that when I hasten towards her,
> it seems to me that I turn backwards
> and that she keeps fleeing from me.[36]

Arnaut Daniel echoes this thought: it is a commonplace that one kills what one desires. This is an important problem, and one that applies to all love poets. Daniel put it like this:

> Tant pan de cor e la queri
> c'ab trop voler cug la'm toll
> s'om ren per ben amar pert.

(I love and desire her so much
from my heart that through too much longing
I think that I rob myself of her, if one can lose anything through loving
truly.)[37]

Courtly love poetry promulgates the cult of the individual. Indeed, some commentators see the rise of personal, individual love as the great contribution of the era: before this age, they claim, love had been impersonal, universal, or at least it had been in art and poetry.[38]

How beautifully we love our beloveds, the troubadours claimed, time after time. Thus Raimbaut d'Aurenga: 'how perfectly I love her'.[39] The more beautiful the desire, the more beautiful the poem, and, ultimately, the more beautiful the artist who made it.

Like God, the beloved woman is not available for interview. We never hear from the adored woman. She is a fabulous object merely, a springboard for the poet's love (and lust). It is the same with the other lyric traditions of the Middle Ages – with the *Minnesängers* of Germany, the *trouvères* of Northern France, the *stil novisti* of Italy, and the Latin lyricists of Europe.

The German *Minnesängers* are often as powerful as the Provençal troubadours – Heinrich von Morungen, Walther von der Vogelweide and Reinnar von Hagenau are some of the well-known poets. Von Morungen wrote:

Si gebiutet und ist in dem herzen min
frowe und herer danne ich selbe si.
(She is in command and more the ruling lady and lord in my heart
more than I am myself.)[40]

Love displaces the psyche of the poet-lover until there is nothing left except love. Hans Denk, the German mystic, said that 'all externals must yield to love.'[41] Some of the mediæval German poets were as intense in their passion as the Sufi mystics:

I renounce all else, I love you with all my heart, you living fountain of the world's delights, I worship you, desire you, seek you, breathlessly follow you, sigh for you to the point of death.[42]

Such passionate lyrics reveal how widespread the courtly love attitudes were: one finds them in the *Carmina Burana,* in vernacular Latin, Icelandic and Spanish lyrics. *Fin amor* was very much an artistic, æsthetic experience. Love, sex and desire were the content, but the form, the shape and the language employed were crucial. Love, sex and desire had and have been around for millions of years. The fusion of love with a highly stylized, ruthlessly controlled stanza form and a language chosen with a meticulous sense of occasion and rightness (not to mention the musical accompaniment) – this was not so much new in the troubadours' poetry as endlessly re-fashioned. For the poets of *fin amor* went over the same ground again and again. They narrowed their poetry into ever tighter and more compressed poems.

Courtly love poetry might end up being decadent, flat and repetitive, if it were not powered by an authentic and intense yearning. This desire, sometimes bitter, sometimes sickly sweet, saves troubadour lyricism from banality and triviality. Although it is the poetry of alienated men wailing like little boys about being all alone and sunk in despair and love-fever, it is nevertheless capable of occasional flights of pure magic.

THREE

&

THE GODDESS OF LOVE

Madonna e disiata in sommo cielo... Dice di lei Amor: 'Cosa mortale
comme esser po si adorna e si pura?!...
(My lady is desired in heaven on high... Love says of her: 'How can
something mortal be so excellent and pure?)

Dante Alighieri, *Vita Nuova* (67)[1]

THE POET AND THE MUSE

Many poets speak of a Muse – Sappho, like many Ancient Greek
poets, had the Goddess Aphrodite, William Shakespeare had his
Dark Lady, John Keats had Fanny Brawne, Charles Baudelaire
had his Black Venus, Robert Herrick had Julia, Samuel Taylor
Coleridge had his Sara ('And I, dear Sara, I am blessing thee!').[2]
The Elizabethan poets exalted women as Diana, Persephone,
Venus, etc. For the *stil novisti*, the Muse was an angel, desexual-
ized, intellectualized, and spiritualized, but still recognisably a
Muse, a Goddess.

It was common for Classical poets to invoke a variety of
Goddesses, while poets of the Middle Ages frequently praised the

Virgin Mary, the *Ave Maria* being just one of thousands of Marian hymns. John Keats wrote passionately of his *belle dame sans merci* (in 'Ode to Melancholy'):

> ...if thy mistress some rich anger shows,
> Emprison her soft hand, and let her rave.
> And feed deep, deep upon her peerless eyes.[3]

Muse poetry is marked by intensity, subjectivity, devotion, sacrality, myth-making, invocation, heterosexuality, veiled eroticism, and magic. The Muse is a powerful presence; the poet must exalt her; her/ his poems nust be as beautiful and exact as possible; becoming enthralled and enslaved by a Muse is exactly like falling in love; Muse poetry is Goddess worship, no question; Muse poetry fuses love, art and religion; the personal becomes the mythic; poets made Goddesses out of women.

There is nothing new, or unusual, in this. Humanity of all ages anthropomorphizes emotions, ideas, and values, until they become deities. Religion began in animism, as E.B. Tylor noted; with shamanism, people became deities, with magical powers. People make other people (or things or animals or symbols) into gods. The Greek pantheon of gods and goddesses are so piquantly, sensually, ironically human. The angry, jealous, solemn God of Judæo-Christian-Islam is like a repressed bureaucrat. God is made in the image of people, not the other way around.

THE GODDESS IN HISTORY

The Goddess can be regarded as an archetype with many aspects, many functions, many attributes and many faces. Earth Goddess figures include the squat stone 'Earth Mothers' of prehistory, the Venuses with no faces and huge hips, such as the Venus of Willendorf. Later, Goddesses came to have names and personalities that are distinctive: Ishtar, Isis, Cerridwen, Sophia, Aphrodite, Diana, Hecate, Medusa, Anu, Maia, Magog, Circe, Io, Minerva, Athena, Brigid and Kali. These Goddesses function as holy Mothers, Mediators, Crones, Lovers, Virgins, Huntresses, Witches and so on. Diana, for instance, is a favourite Goddess of Francesco Petrarch's – the huntress Diana, virginal, fierce, associated with the sharp blade of the crescent moon, the Goddess that Actæon saw bathing naked (later, Diana was taken up by followers of witchcraft). Daphne is another beloved Goddess of Petrarch's, the deity who changed into a laurel tree to escape the lust of Apollo in Ovid's *Metamorphoses*.

Many Goddesses are extraordinarily powerful. Some are creators of the world. In the *Homeric Hymns* the Goddess Aphrodite is 'the richest force on earth',[4] while Joseph Campbell calls the Goddess 'time and space itself... everything is within her' (in *The Power of Myth*, 167). This view sees the Goddess's body as the world, the cosmos. The Goddess is thus the Great Mother of All Things, who gave birth to everything. Ancient poets said of the Goddess Ishtar: 'She is glorious',[5] and indeed she was.

Even the Virgin Mary, a seemingly passive and watered down, desexualized version of Isis and Diana, was called 'the Queen of Heaven and Earth', the Star of the Sea, the Mediatrix, the Primum Mobile, the Magna Mater, the Plenum. The Goddess is the Great Round, the Mistress of All, the Mother of the Dead and the Origin of All Life.

In modern times the Goddess has been studied and exalted by poets and thinkers such as Lynnie Levy, J.J. Bachofen, Robert

Briffault, Robert Graves, Ean Begg, Peter Redgrove, Monica Sjöo, Shirley Nicholson, Barbara Walker, Marion Woodman, Merlin Stone, Esther Harding, Marina Warner, Elinor Gadon, Erich Neumann, Marija Gimbutas and O. Crawford. The Goddess is seen as the 'I-Dea', the Goddess Within, a nurturing, empowering figure, the potential for re-birth and a renewal of life.[6] Feminists, neo-pagans and artists are re-claiming the Goddess: they speak of a holistic vision, one world, the Gaia-consciousness, the 'global Goddess'.[7]

This new Goddess is earthy, sexual, gentle, radical, magical and eco-friendly. But the same glorification of women is at work here as in the art of the troubadours, in Dante Alighieri and Francesco Petrarch.

THE GODDESS IN POETRY

The poet plays the role of the Goddess's lover – like the consorts of ancient mythologies: Tammuz with Ishtar, Osiris with Isis, Orpheus with Eurydice, Taliessin with Cerridwen, even Jesus with Mary. The Goddess becomes the spirit of poetry itself, or art, or the embodiment of a nation (think of the French with their Victory figures, or America with its Statue of Liberty).

The troubadours spoke of the 'Lord of Love', but behind that deity was the Goddess. The Eternal Feminine is a better description of the Lord of Love. The characteristics of the deity Love in courtly love poetry is that of a Goddess; she is often cruel – so many troubadours bewail the cruelty of their lady. This is the Goddess as a killer, a *femme fatale* – Hecate, Medusa, Kali, Cerridwen.

Examples in literature include William Shakespeare's 'Dark Lady' and the vampiric woman of Romantic and Decadent art (in the art of John Keats, Charles Baudelaire, Gustave Moreau, Félicien Rops, Franz von Stück, etc). For the Romantics, she was the 'Lady of Pain', the ghostly, white-faced 'Nightmare Life-in-Death' as Samuel Taylor Coleridge put it.[8]

By projecting their frustrations onto a Goddess figure, the poets tried to find a way out of self-hatred, ambiguity, confusion, doubt, difficulty and solitude. The image of the unkind Goddess is, ultimately, just another way in which men try to transcend the harsh realities of the human condition.

The Sex or Love Goddess is a familiar figure. In modern times, movie stars and celebrities have fulfilled many of the mythic, functions of the ancient Sex Goddess (Marilyn Monroe, Brigitte Bardot, Sophia Loren, Scarlett Johanssen, etc). The Goddess as Mother too is familiar – it is one of the few functions which the Virgin Mary was allowed to retain. Desexualized, the Madonna is still sensual in her motherhood. Mystics such as St Bernard eroticized the Madonna – St Bernard even received milk from her breast (a ridiculous moment, especially when it is depicted in paintings: the saint kneels, arms wide in adoration, while the Virgin squirts a stream of milk at him.) The Mother figure at least has some positive aspects – there is life in her, unlike the Cruel Goddess, who embodies the usual patriarchal notions of sex, pain and death.

The Elizabethan era produced many Muse poets in Great Britain: Sir Thomas Wyatt, Edmund Spenser, Thomas Canpion, Sir Philip Sidney, Michael Drayton and Samuel Daniel. The poems of the Elizabethan Age develop the sequences of courtly love, drawing heavily on the troubadours and Francesco Petrarch and the sonnet form: *To Delia* (Daniel), *Diana* (Constable), *Idea* (Drayton), *Amoretti* (Spenser) and *Astrophel and Stella* (Sidney).

In Europe, other love poem sequences pivot around the pleasures and pains of the Goddess's love: Torquato Tasso's *Rime*, Maurice Scève's *Délie*, Pierre Ronsard's *Sonnets For Hélène*, and lyrics by François Villon, Charles d'Orleans and Joachim du Bellay. In the courtly love epoch, Goddess worship seems as widespread as orthodox Christianity. Meister Eckhart speaks of the mystic being 'God-Intoxicated', and many poets of the European Middle Ages appeared to be 'Goddess-intoxicated'. In the *Carmina Burana* we read 'Fervens illamea/ ignis est' ('She is my fire, blazing'), and

> per quem mestus vigeo,
> et gaudeo,
> illam pre cunctis diligo
> veneror ut deam
> (she for whose sake I live in joy and grief, colouring her as goddess
> whom I love beyond all love)[9]

The devotion of poets to their beloved lady, like that of the mystic to God or the Catholic monk or nun to the Madonna, verges on the psychotic. We read in a poem by Sordello, one of the later (Italian) troubadours:

> Lady Delightful, root of all merit, I am in heart, in body, and in deeds
> and words entirely yours, for you are the most perfect, pure and
> pleasing, gentle and discerning.[10]

The Goddess, in all her aspects, demands absolute loyalty from her subjects. The scenario seems to be the feudal one of lord and vassal, but in fact the master-and-slave configuration is ancient in poetry and mythology. The cults of Isis, Ishtar, Demeter and Venus were as rigorous ritually and psychologically. One recalls the relationship between Apuleius and Isis in *The Golden Ass*, for instance. Isis was (and is) the incredibly powerful Goddess who for a 'while was pure magic'. Unveiled, Isis was the Mother of All. She had the magic of language inside her, the power of the Creative Word:

> I am Isis the Goddess and I am the Lady of the Words of Power, and I
> know how to work with words of power, and most mighty are my
> Words![11]

The Goddess of the mediæval troubadours is a distant lady, a Muse who is and is not a real person. In Robert Graves' mythology of the poetic Muse, she can be incarnated in a real person – the Goddess 'rides' the Muse woman. Graves' mythology of Muse poetry is a modern version of courtly love. Though the relationship is distant and basically spiritual, there is always an erotic component, as there is in the relation between the troubadour and her/ his Muse.

The troubadours always stay this side of the earthly; their charged eroticism remains unsublimated in many cases. In mysticism, sex is typically sublimated into spiritual feeling; this is true of the *stil novisti*. The Elizabethans turned round the excessive piety of mediæval verse and put the pagan, sexual element back into poetry. The Romantics exaggerated Renaissance sensuality, but like the troubadours they continued to make mythologies out of love-pain. The Goddess appears on the surface or underneath much of Romantic lyricism – certainly in the poetry of Percy Shelley, Lord Byron, John Clare, Samuel Coleridge, Charles Baudelaire, Novalis, and Johann Wolfgang von Goethe ('In your name, MOTHERS!', Goethe wrote in *Faust* [III, 521]).

Among later poets, among those who invoke the Goddess and use Goddess-related imagery and themes and who move towards a new invocation of the Eternal Feminine, some of the most typical are Paul Éluard, Robert Graves, D.H. Lawrence, Gabriele d'Annunzio, Adrienne Rich and Emily Dickinson.

Love as a theme and prime emotion was overshadowed in the modern era by the formal experiments and abstractions of T.S. Eliot and Ezra Pound. But there are today hundreds of poets, women poets especially, who write powerfully and lucidly about erotic and emotional experiences. They are the inheritors of a love poetry tradition which is really not tradition at all, but a vague shorthand of the historian for a multiplicity of cultural movements. Love poets write not out of traditions, but from their personal experiences, although of course their society and enculturation shapes their expressions and forms. The universality of the love experience enables Sappho to be read as if her fragments were written in the last few minutes, rather than over two thousand years ago.

FOUR

❧

DANTE AND BEATRICE

And when it pleases that One who is the Lord of Graciousness that my soul ascend to behold the glory of its lady, that is, of that blessed Beatrice, who in glory gazes upon the countenance of the One *who is through all ages blessed.*

Dante Alighieri, *Vita Nuova,* XLII (84)

THE SWEET NEW STYLE

In his *Ars Amatoria*, Ovid wrote that 'tender love must be nurtured with sweet words'.[1] Sweetness is one of the hallmarks of the *canzoni* of the Italian *dolce stil novo* poets. Their poetry is severely etherealized, rarefied, intellectualized and spiritualized. The sweetness of the key poets, Guido Guinicelli, Cino da Pistoia, Onesto da Bologna, Guido Cavalcanti and Dante Alighieri himself is often too much: it becomes sickly. The 'sweet new style' (*dolce stil novo*) is like a bunch of lilies: the flowers are beautiful, especially in so many Annunciation paintings, but too many of them, for too long, are too much. Similarly, with the Early Renaissance paintings of Fra Filippo Lippi, Fra Angelico and

Sandro Botticelli – all those coy, wan Madonnas looking demurely at the floor while some peacock-winged archangel offers than a bunch of lilies.

Such imagery can become too much for some. It is too sweet, too contrived, too constrained. Such aching towards perfection becomes deathly. In the *dolce stil novo,* art becomes over-refined. Art becomes artifice, and nothing else. Life gets smothered under a gorgeous surface gloss of exquisite, poetic flourishes.

At its best, the *dolce stil novo* is a poetry full of light, an airy, bright style, as when Guido Guinicelli writes: 'I think her radiance passes all that's bright'.[2] When it soars like this, the Italian new sweet style reads as authentic poetry, a poetry which balances dazzling word magic with deep emotional experiences.

The poets of the Italian *dolce stil novo* emphasized the idealized, gentle, courteous aspects of courtly love. Sexuality is sidestepped in favour of pure desire. Yearning becomes an end in itself: there is no promise of sex with the beloved. The lady instead becomes a springboard for restrained and refined musings on the state of being in love. The woman is denied; she vanishes, as Maurice Valency noted.[3] The refinements of the soul replace the burning passion of the heart.

It is not all sickly-sweet, however: Dante Alighieri, far and away the finest of the *stil novisti* (and the best-known today, of course), is fiery and fierce at times – in his *Rime petrose,* for instance, which celebrates a cruel, hardy, stony love affair.

If the troubadours seemed to stoop low before their beloved woman, the *stil novisti* fall flat on the ground in a swoon. They faint with love-sickness like the heroines of some 18th century comedy of manners, or the aristocratic æsthetes in a Parisian café *circa* 1885. The new sweet style poet is more than a little like the anti-heroes of Decadent literature – like Des Esseintes, for instance, in J.-K. Huysman's *À Rebours,* who sinks into luxurious self-absorption. Like Narcissus staring at himself in the pool, the *stil novisti* stare at their souls and weep.

They are terrified of their beloveds – the look of the woman now kills, not wounds. The look of the basilisk animal kills, in mediæval legend, and the way to fight a basilisk was to take a mirror and let it look at itself. The *stil novisti* poets instead stare at themselves, at their souls reflected in the mirror of their poems, but they don't die. The adored women often die – like Beatrice, for instance.

In death, Beatrice is beatified; and, by the connections of æsthetics, the poet is also glorified. It is the same with Laura in Francesco Petrarch's poetic cycle: she dies and is exalted, but it is the poet, Petrarch, who receives the richer glory.

Denying the flesh, sexuality and the body is one of the main psychological strains of Christianity. 'Christianity associated the sexual act with evil, sin, the Fall and death', as Michel Foucault put it.[4]

The *stil novisti* expunge sexuality and write in an intellectual, scholastic and theological fashion. Their language is that of the Christian theologian, of Thomas Aquinas and St Augustine. As with Francesco Petrarch, there is an emphasis on the eyes and the face of the beloved. The rest of her body remains vaguely sketched. Like monks, the *stil novisti* live alone in ascetic abstinence, chaste, virginal, pure, but yearning.

BEATRICE THE ANGEL

In the dark alleys of mediæval Florence, Dante Alighieri first beheld his beloved Beatrice Portinari. Her historical reality has been debated, but clearly Dante considered his love for her as real enough. There are moments in the *Vita Nuova* and *The Divine Comedy* that suggest a real, human love affair, rather than an ethereal romance with an angel. There is the poet's dream, for instance, in the *Vita Nuova*: the imagery of the dream is typically

Christian and romantic: the fire, the red dress, the heart, the burning sensation. It is a highly erotic dream, too – Beatrice is naked under the 'crimson cloth', and the dream ends with an act of oral eroticism: Love gives Dante-poet's 'burning heart' to Beatrice, and she eats it. Sigmund Freud would have a field day with such a dream. No commentators have mentioned the menstrual nature of the Dante-poet's dream: Beatrice, for instance, wears a blood-red dress (*Vita Nuova,* 4), which is symbolic of menstruation as well as the Christian Passion.

For a time in the *Vita Nuova,* Dante Alighieri's poet's love of Beatrice Portinari has an erotic element. Like any courtly love poet, he trembles violently when he sees her. But distance creeps in: soon it is the memory of her that fires him up, as with Francesco Petrarch's remembrances of Laura de Sade (*Vita Nuova,* 29).

Dante Alighieri's poet becomes a slave to Love (59), but Beatrice becomes ever more distant. The Dantean poet can only look at her from afar. This is the classic situation of courtly *amor de lonh*. There is no exchange of sensual touches: Dante's poet hovers about, sighing woefully. He wallows in his holy martyrdom of love. He stresses the honesty and nobility of his loving and his undertaking of adoring the blessed woman. But he remains curiously impotent and ineffectual. After he's seen her, he scurries back to his rooms and writes a poem about it.

After a while it becomes clear in *Vita Nuova* that this is as much a literary record as an emotional one. With the Italian *stil novisti*, art triumphs over raw emotion: emotion gets squeezed out and the æsthetics of pleasure shift and become the æsthetics of æsthetics, art about art.

It is clear that Beatrice in Dante Alighieri's *New Life* is an excuse for self-indulgent poeticizing. The woman, the relationship, the nuances of sensuality and circumstance are transcended, or subverted, in favour of a poetry that exalts the art of poetry, memory and refinement itself.

Dante Alighieri has 'cast over the inherited eroticism of the tradition a veil of Christian mystic significance', as Thomas Bergin put it in *Dante's Divine Comedy* (12). In this Christianized lyricism, women become angels, as in Guido Cavalcanti's "Yeggio negli occhi", where the woman dazzles him.₅ These angelic women make people gasp when they walk by; they are radiant; their eyes kill; they outshine the sun; they are superhuman.

Critics complain that the portrait of Beatrice in the *Vita Nuova* is fuzzy, vague. But this is so Dante A. can transform her into an angel. If he had drawn her portrait full of imperfections – a hairy top lip, warts, a tick in the left eye, an uneven hairline, pasty skin, ill-fitting clothes and so on, it would have been much more difficult for us to believe she had become an angel.

And Beatrice is more than an angel, too. Angels are messengers, sparks of light, splinters of God, beings of speed and violence who exist somewhere between here and there, Heaven and Earth. Beatrice is more than the *donna angelicata,* she becomes a special kind of guide who can traverse the whole of Heaven. In becoming pure blessedness, pure spirit and pure beauty, Beatrice leaves Earth and ascends to Heaven to be one of the guides on the magical mystery tour of Dante's *Divina Commedia*.

THE DIVINE COMEDY

Dante Alighieri's great poem, *The Divine Comedy*, is an attempt at an all-inclusive view of the world and everything in it. It is regarded as the culmination of mediæval thought and life, the apotheosis of the last great religious age in the Western world. It is basically a vision quest in the shamanic tradition, where Virgil plays the shaman who can travel to other worlds and guide souls to their resting place.

At times, *The Divine Comedy* reveals a cranky, mechanical

picture of the world – some cosmic machine with the chunks of Aristotle, Plato, theology and poetry fitted in with bolts and bits of string, powered by a clockwork motor called Love (and with God of course at the centre). You can almost hear the whirr of the flywheels and the gears as the planets zoom around the heavens in Dante's poem. One is reminded of those clockwork models of the Solar System made of shiny brass where the (known) planets rotate around the sun on lengths of wire and rods.

Dante Alighieri's *Divine Comedy* is a mass of lore, science, occultism, numerology, astrology, cosmology and philosophy. It is all held together by the all-pervading energy of God. But if one doesn't accept that element, that attempt at producing a cosmic unity, then *The Divine Comedy* turns out to be a ragbag collection of different philosophies, a syncretic mixture that seldom gels together. The worldview in *The Divine Comedy* is seething with a multiplicity of beliefs and images – as varied as the philosophies of second century Alexandria.

Poetically, *The Divine Comedy* is remarkable, no question. The visions are often stunning: the largest work in literature, for instance – the Mystic Rose. It is wonderful to see the angelic hierarchies of Dionysius the Areopagite used to such startling effect. The image of God surrounded by the angelic multitude is truly spectacular.

The poem is suffused with light in the third book, *Paradise*. Many times light floods the scene: the immense light helps to give Dante Alighieri's poem the edge of authentic mysticism:

I saw a great expanse of Heaven ablaze
with the sun's flames.
(*Paradise*, I, 79-80)

The Divine Comedy is a series of revelations, a journey from one revelation to another. The poet is very aware of piling on the literary fireworks: each sunburst must be more dazzling than the one before. The poem is a quest, an exploration, a mythical journey, in an archetypal Western fashion.

But also it is one revelation extended over hundreds of pages and thousands of *terza rima*. The revelation is of everything – all at once. Dante Alighieri simply unravels the revelation, splitting it up into sections, giving it rhythm, form, symbolism and philosophy.

The most spectacular descriptions of the nine tiers of angels surrounding God is undoubtedly Dante Alighieri's *Paradiso*, which seems beyond visual illustration (though Gustave Doré has come closest, and Sandro Botticelli produced a beautiful interpretation of Dante's epic poem):

> From choir to choir I heard Hosanna rolled
> To that fixed Point which holds them in their home,
> Hath held them ever, and shall forever hold.
> (*Paradiso*, Canto XXVIII, 94-96)

One of the most influential of early Christian texts is *The Celestial Hierarchies* by Dionysus the Areopagite, also known as the Pseudo-Dionysus (a theologian of Athens), written around the 1st century A.D. (it was about the celestial hierarchies of the angels in heaven):

> We have agreed that the most venerable Hierarchy of the Intelligences, which is close to God, is consecrated by His first and highest Ray, and uplifting itself directly to It, is purified, illuminated and perfected by the Light of the Godhead which is both hidden and more revealed.
> (1965)

Beatrice Portinari has many things to do in *The Divine Comedy*, where before (in the *Vita Nuova*), she had been merely a beautiful object. More than an angel, she is clearly a Goddess, equated with Sophia, but modelled more on the Virgin Mary.

It would be blasphemous for Dante Alighieri to place his woman next to Mary and Christ, but half of him wishes to do so. Sane of the best moments and the best lines in *The Divine Comedy* concern Beatrice or are spoken by Beatrice, such as this from Canto XXX:

"We have gone beyond –
the greatest sphere to heaven of pure light,
light of the intellect, light full of love,
love of the true good, full of ecstasy,
ecstasy that transcends the sweetest joy." (38-42)

In Dante Alighieri's work, the beloved lady is 'transformed from a term of desire into an active prize, a 'beatrice'', remarked Patrick Boyde in *Dante's Style In His Lyric Poetry* (172). In Beatrice, Dante Alighieri combines the earthly and the heavenly, so that Beatrice is simultaneously an angel and an earthly woman. In Beatrice, sex and religion fuse: she is the Portinari of Florence, in a crimson dress, and very much desired by the poet, and she is also Sophia or Sapientia, a spiritual apotheosis.

Art, love and religion unite. What unites them is the transformative powers of the poet. Critic William Anderson (in *Dante the Maker*), sees Beatrice as the culmination of the troubadours' beloved, Dante Alighieri's philosophical reading, his spiritual and artistic development, and his *dolce stil novo* predilections (141).

Beatrice at times becomes Love itself, the projected desires of the yearning Dante-poet. As Charles Singleton put it in *An Essay On the Vita Nuova*, 'Beatrice remains… Beatrice is Love. And Beatrice remains to the end' (174). For some critics, the *fedeli d'amore* (Guido Cavalcanti *et al*) used a secret language to protect their sect from being found out as a heresy – a Sophia cult, perhaps.[6] But the secret language – of names, numbers, dates, anniversaries (the number nine in Dante's poetry, the number six in Francesco Petrarch's work) – is more probably (and rightly) the creation of the poet, part of her/ his personal mythology of love.

Dante Alighieri is mystical: no amount of his classy, self-conscious poeticizing can hide the deep mystical feelings underneath. With the other *stil novlsti*, the angelization of the woman becomes repetitive, and self-parodic.

With Dante Alighieri, the intensity of his feeling transcends the sweet style of his poetry. Meeting Beatrice was a 'mystical experience of enhanced consciousness' (D. Singleton, 40), culminating in the highpoints of *The Divine Comedy*: for instance, 18:20-21, 21:1-8, 23:70f, 31:91-92.

Beatrice is the mediator for Dante Alighieri who moves between the poet and God. Through her he understands the infinity and splendour of God's plan, the whole cosmological view which opens out so magnificently in *The Divine Comedy*. It is all reflected in Beatrice face:

> for the Eternal Joy was shining straight into my Beatrice's face, and back came its reflection filling me with joy. (*Paradiso*, 18:16-18)

Petrarch (below).
Manuscript by Petrarch
(left, found in 1985).

Portraits of Francesco Petrarch
(this page and over)

FRANCISCVS PETRARCHA

Giorgio Vasari, Six Tuscan Poets, 1544, Minneapolis

Laura de Sade

Josef Manes, Laura and Petrarch, 1845

Philippe-Jacques van Breé, Laure et Pétrarque à Fontaine de Vaucluse

Andrea del Castagno, Dante Alighieri, 1450,
Uffizi Gallery, Florence

Luca Signorell, Dante, fresco, Orvieto Cathedral

Elisabeth Sonrel, Scenes From Dante Alighieri's Vita Nuova

Sandro Botticelli, The Map of Hell, 1480-90, Vatican

Antonio Cotti, Dante In Verona, 1879, Lyon

Eugène Delacroix, The Barque of Dante,
1822, Louvre

Eugene-Auguste-Francois Deully, Dante and Virgil in Hell, 1897

Enrico Pazzi, Dant Alighieri, 1875, Santa Croce

Rafael Flores, Dante and Virgil Visiting the Inferno,
1855, Mexico City

Andrea Pierini, Dante alla corte di Guido Novello,
1855, Florence

Dante Gabriel Rossetti, Dante's Dream At the Time of the Death
of Beatrice, 1871, Walker Art Gallery

Dante Gabriel Rossetti, Beata Beatrix, 1864-70, Tate Britain

Marie Spartall Stillman, Beatrice, 1915

John William Waterhouse, Dante and Matilda, 1915,
Dahesh Museum of Art

Illustrations for The Divine Comedy by Gustave Doré

Gustave Doré, Dante and Beatrice, from The Divine Comedy

Troubadours in mediæval manuscripts
(this page and over).

Examples of courtly love.

Arnaut Daniel

The Romance of the Rose (above).
Peire Vidal (below).

Bernard de Ventadour

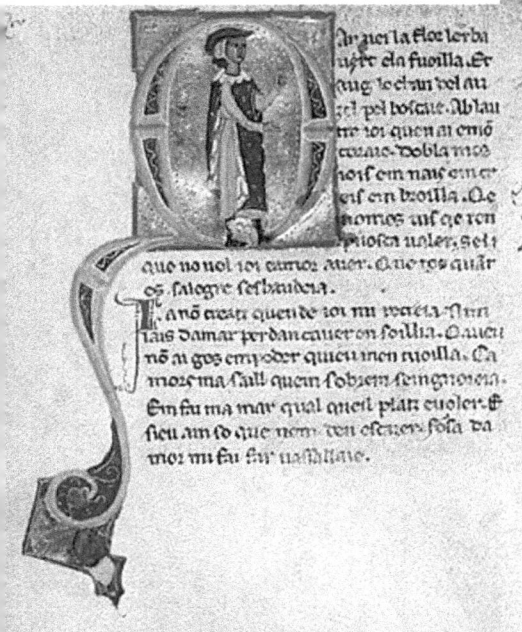

Bertran de Born (above).
Peire d'Alvernhe (below).

PER TUTTI I CERCHI DEL DOLENTE REGNO,
RISPOSE ELLI, SON IO DI QUA VENUTO.
Purgatorio c. VII v. 22 e 23

Gustave Doré, Dante With Sordello

Federico Faruffini, Sordello and Cunizza, 1864 (above).
Pierre-Henri Révoil, René d'Anjou At Palamè de Forbin, 1820 (below).

The garden from Andreas Capellanus, The Art of Courtly Love

Henri Martin, L'apparition de Clémence Isaure aux Troubadours, 1898.

FIVE

❧

LAURA

Erano i capei d'oro a l'aura sparsi
che 'n mille dolci nodi git avolgea,
e 'l vago lume oltra misura ardea
di quei begli occhi, ch' or ne son si scarsi;

e 'l viso di pietosi color farsi
(non so se vero o falso) mi parea;
i' che l'esca amorosa al petto avea,
qual meraviglia se di subito arsi?

Non era l'andar suo cosa mortale
ma d'angelica forma, et le parole
sonavan altro che pur voce umana:

umo spirito celeste, mi vivo sole
fu quel ch' i' vidi, et se non fosse or tale,
piaga per allentar d'arco non sana.

(Her golden hair was loosed to the breeze, which turned it in a
thousand sweet knots, and the lovely light burned without measure in
her eyes, which are now so stingy of it; and it seemed to me (I know
not whether truly or falsely) her face took on the color of pity: I, who
had the tinder of love in my breast, what wonder is it if I suddenly
caught fire? Her walk was not that of a mortal thing but of some
angelic form, and her words sounded different from a merely human
voice: a celestial spirit, a living sun was what I saw, and if she were
not such now, a wound is not healed by the loosening of the bow.)

Francesco Petrarch, *Rime Sparse* (all of sonnet 90)

LAURA, THE APOTHEOSIS OF COURTLY LOVE

Francesco Petrarch's Laura de Sade is the apotheosis of the courtly love *donna* and the angel of the Italian *dolci stil novo*. The troubadours exalted women in mythic terms, but they remained earthly women. There was always the hope of a sexual consummation with the beloved, and the beloveds resided in courts and castles, in cities and recognizably earthly places. The angelic madonnas of the *stil novisti* exist in a timeless space, an idealized garden somewhere; the angelized women of the Italian poets have just descended from Heaven – they have just stepped of an earthbound cloud:

> Her human visage, like an angel's made.
> (Tommaso Buzzola de Faenza)[1]

Beatrice joined together the erotic woman of courtly love with spiritual soul of Christianity.[2] Similarly with Francesco Petrarch's Laura. She is both mortal beauty, prone to decay, and a celestial spirit, who rejoices in timeless beauty. Petrarch was never quite able to resolve the conflicts between the earthly and the heavenly Laura. He loved both, needed both and manufactured both in his *Canzoniere*.

Francesco Petrarch's *Canzoniere* is the most intense, lyrical and extended exaltation of a beloved in poetry. No other poet seems to have spent so much time and energy exalting one person. Dune's Beatrice is like a female saint: a 'mirror of Christ'. In a similar fashion, Beatrice and Laura are mirrors of the poet's desire. Many critics say that in eulogizing Laura, Petrarch is eulogizing himself. This is true. The *Rime Sparse* is a tremendously self-conscious work, and the poet dwells upon himself obsessively.

LAURA THE WOMAN

What we know of Laura de Sade the actual person (a.k.a. Laura de Noves, wife of the Count Hugues de Sade), is as scant as our knowledge of Beatrice Portinari. But such a long and complex sequence of poems all aimed at one woman does not come from nowhere. Francesco Petrarch's *Rime Sparse* is as deeply founded in an actual experience of love as any love poem – as with the lyrics of Sappho, Catullus, William Shakespeare, or Paul Éluard.

Whether Laura was real or not makes no difference at all to the magic of the *Rime Sparse*. What is real is Francesco Petrarch's experience of her, his endless poeticizing of her, his obsession with her, his lust for her, his hatred of her and his desire for transcendence through her.

She was born in 1310 and died in 1348. When Petrarch met her in Avignon in 1327, she was 16 or 17. Her father was Audibert de Noves, a knight, and her mother was Ermessenda. Laura married Count Hugues de Noves on Jan 16, 1325 (aged 15 – so she was already wed when Petrarch met her). According to the legend of Petrarch, one of the reasons that the poet stayed in Avignon, and later came back to live in the Vaucluse, was to be near Laura. The poet Maurice Scève (a devoted Petrarchan) claimed to have found her tomb in 1533.

Francesco Petrarch was concerned that Laura should not be regarded as a poetic creation merely. In his letter of 1336 to Giascomo Colonna he said:

> What then do you say? That I have invented the lovely name of "Laura" in order to have someone to talk about, and in order to set people talking about me, but that, in truth, I have no "Laura" in mind, except that poetic laurel to which I have aspired, as my long and untiring study bears witness. But, believe me, it takes much trouble to keep up a pretence for long…[3]

Laura hardly exists at all in historical documents,[4] but Francesco Petrarch thought her existence essential to the authority of his poetic enterprise. If Laura is bogus, a pretence, his love and his poetry becomes weakened. The name itself, 'Laura' (variations include Laurea, Aurora, Laureta), is a code name, a *senhal*. Giovanni Boccaccio had his Flammetta ('small flame'), Cino da Pistoia his Salvaggia ('the wild one'), and Dante his Beatrice ('she who blesses').

The name *Laura* was of immense significance to Francesco Petrarch. It was a holy name, endlessly played with in the poems: as *auro* = gold, *aura* = dawn/ breeze, *aurato* = gilded, *aureo* = golden, *lauro* = laurel, *aurora* = dawn, and so on.

One recalls that the names of deities were sacred things in themselves. To speak a deity's name is itself a holy act, whether the deity be *Pan, Aphrodite, Baphomet, Buddha, Allah* or *Krishna*. The word 'Laura' was magical for Francesco Petrarch – all the more so because it was bound up with his deep concerns for poetic fame, embodied in the 'laurel' of Roman emperors and crowned poets.

LAURA AS POETIC CREATION

Laura is a poetic creation. What we know of her comes from the poems, the treatises, the letters, the ecologues, and the *Triumphs* of Francesco Petrarch. What we know of her, in short, is all Petrarch wishes us to know about her. Petrarch is a clever, self-aware poet. One senses that he is continually editing everything he writes in order to preserve exactly the right image of Laura (and also the portrait of himself) for posterity. Reading Petrarch's work, we must always remember that he is writing for future fame. Like André Gide, Petrarch shapes his writing to suit his notions of what culture will value now and in the (in his) future. Petrarch is the sort of writer who will not simply 'suppress' certain writings: he will go outside and burn them himself, to make sure they disappear forever.

'Image' – the word, in the 21st century, has come to connote a self-conscious obsession with presentation, with the 'image' presented to an audience, a certain affectation or pretentiousness. We find this in Francesco Petrarch's art. He is ever conscious of posterity. He exalts the authors of the past – Cicero, Virgil, St Augustine – and he knows they survive because of their finely controlled prose.

At the same time, Francesco Petrarch's *Rerum vulgarum fragmenta* is a collection of passionate lyrics which show that the poet was consumed by desire for his beloved Laura. The deep emotion burns through, time after time, and the whole sequence makes sense as a love poem – that is, a construct which is powered by love-pain but is also a poem, a literary production, a conceit, an artifice. In Petrarch's output, it is impossible to separate love from art. Love and art are twins born in the womb of the poet's creativity, and they will not be split apart at the point of delivery, or even after they've grown up.

Obsessed by Laura, Francesco Petrarch could not escape her nor transcend her. Even that final, ecstatic hymn to the Blessed Virgin Mary, at the end of the *Rime Sparse,* is unconvincing after hundreds of poems directed at Laura the mortal (though angelic) woman. The self-transcendence of the poet is only partial. In a letter of 1338 (to Giacomo Colonna), which could have been written much later, Petrarch said

> Still she stands before my eyes, terrifying me, assailing me, nor does she show any sign of leaving me in peace. She had captured me by no feminine gifts, but by her simple ways and by her rare beauty.[5]

LAURA THE GODDESS

Time after time in the *Rime Sparse,* Laura is exalted as a Goddess: she is Daphne, Diana, Medusa, Echo, Danæ, and the Virgin Mary. Laura functions as a classic Muse: she is cruel, ambivalent, demands loyalty and asceticism, and is beguilingly beautiful. Francesco Petrarch feels he has to praise her endlessly to satisfy her. Her desire (his desire projected) is voracious. When his poetic desire is in its Augustinian, theological mood, it demands ever purer poetry where sin is loathed and transcended; but there is a pagan, sensual side to Petrarch's poetic personality: when this aspect is in the ascendant (where Venus, the Goddess of Love, is rising, we might say), his poetry 'falls' into sensuality. Here, the Angel Laura lures him like a siren of old, like the archetypal Fatal Woman, and he is both fascinated and repulsed.

The slide into sensuality is a 'fall' because Francesco Petrarch continually revaluates his experiences in *Christian* terms. Thus some former sensual occurrence is in the future given a Christian interpretation. The conscience of the poet, embodied in the figure of St Augustine, the stern father figure, criticizes earlier emotions. Love becomes a 'lapse', equivalent of the Fall of Adam and Eve.

In this fiercely chauvinist and archaic scenario, Eve is blamed for Adam's fall into temptation. The language of the *Bible* at this point in *Genesis* is extremely woman-hating. Eve is seen as the seductress that ruined humankind. Such a view is plainly mistaken, but the later Christian Fathers acknowledged this view, and developed it even further. The early Christian theologian Tertullian said of women:

> You are the devil's gateway, you desecrated the fatal tree, you first betrayed the law of God...[6]

For St Augustine, we are born 'between urine and fæces', an extraordinary phrase which summarizes his particular hatred of the flesh, of sex, of women, of earthly life. Augustine is a major influence on Francesco Petrarch. He is the one who interrogates the poet in the *Secretum*, where the poet tries to defend himself against Augustine's charges.

The whole Christian argument of sin, vice, concupiscence, fall and death is formidable in its forceful denial of life, yet it was so powerful and influential – at least up until the Middle Ages and the time of Francesco Petrarch, Dante Alighieri and the troubadours.

Another of Francesco Petrarch's influences, St John Chrysostom, wrote:

> The whole of her bodily beauty is nothing less than phlegm, blood, bile, rheum, and the fluid of digested blood.[7]

This anti-women thinking occurs throughout the *Canzoniere* of Francesco Petrarch. In the lyrics, though, it is disguised as anti-sensuality, anti-human love. By attacking Love, the poet seems to be excusing himself from attacking women. But the two – women and erotic love – are bound up together. To lay into one is to attack the other.

The *Rime Sparse*, however, is not one long sequence of loathing of love. First the poet has to build up a mythology of love, in which love and Love are celebrated. This is one of the things Francesco Petrarch is best at: an ironic, self-deprecating but also ecstatic celebration of love.

INCARNATIONS OF LAURA

Each critic writes her/ his own 'Laura', just as s/he writes her/ his own 'Petrarch'. Most critics are male (or masculinist/ patriarchal, if not gendered male), though the consumers of the *Rime Sparse* are male and female: but when the critic writes her/ his own Laura, s/he creates a Laura out of her/ his own enculturation and experience. We end up with a Laura who accords very much with patriarchal values and attitudes towards women. Laura's a masculine construct, in the poems and in the literary criticism (like the Virgin Mary). Laura is an idealized feminine spirit, the soul-image of centuries of (mainly male) critics.

Laura is thus like a million objects of (masculine) desire: Cleopatra, Héloise, Joan of Arc, Catherine the Great, Venus, Kali, Isis, Ishtar, Inanna – real women made mythical Goddesses made out of amalgamations of male feelings about women. Men create these women and Goddesses – edit and shape them, censor and silence them.

Poetry or pornography? Pornography is the objectification and graphic depiction of female sexually, and poetry adds to this objectification and sexualized depiction.[8] Francesco Petrarch's *Rime Sparse* and Dante Alighieri's *Vita Nuova* are regarded as the highpoints of Western poetry, along with the works of Torquato Tasso, Maurice Scève, John Milton, Johann Wolfgang von Goethe and Victor Hugo. But Dante's and Petrarch's works are poems that (re-)affirm all of the values and attitudes of patriarchy (how could it be otherwise?). Everything that men love women to be, we find in the poetic figures of Beatrice and Laura. Everything, that is, except the portrayal of women as whores (Petrarch and Dante keep their beloveds on the side of virgins not whores). In the work of Petrarch and Dante, sexuality is sublimated, transformed into spirituality.

This sublimation is seen at its most obvious in the mediæval era in St Bernard's rewriting of the *Song of Songs*, a blatantly erotic work (Marina Warner says that '[t]here has never been a more intense communication of the experience of desire').[9]

What saves the poetry of Dante Alighieri and Francesco Petrarch and the troubadours from being regarded as pornography is art: the subtlety, skill, power and magic of their poetry. Their work may be pornographic, but this is ignored by critics who see only great art. Great their art certainly is, but we should never forget that their depiction of women is also narrow, often shallow, limiting, chauvinist and sometimes psychotic and childish. Of course, we do not expect Dante, Petrarch or any writer, male or female, to be a feminist in the modern sense in the mediæval era (though some were – Hildegard of Bingen, for instance, and some of the female troubadours).

Dante Alighieri and Francesco Petrarch are successful partly because of the structure of literary criticism, which is patriarchal, reflecting the society it caters for. Critics are still mostly male (or masculine): the emotions in the works of Petrarch and Dante chime with those of masculinist culture. The same celebration of women writers is very rare: one thinks of the Brontës, Jane Austen and Virginia Woolf among British artists. But these women writers are not as highly regarded (generally) as Dante, Petrarch, Shakespeare, Donne, Joyce, Eliot, Hugo, Goethe, Mann or Whitman.

Francesco Petrarch's *Canzoniere* (a.k.a. 'My Love Affair with Laura') was written with a male-oriented audience in mind. Petrarch's patriarchal attitudes are seen in his acquaintances and friendships – the Popes, kings, bishops and noblemen. We know little to nothing, for example, about Petrarch's son's mother. The only woman who features prominently is Laura, and she is vaguely described. The details of her life, her relationships, her family, her history, her views, values and attitudes are left out of the *Rime Sparse*, as with Beatrice in the *Vita Nuova*. Instead, we are invited by by Petrarch to construct the woman from the poetry, and the few other places where she appears.

PORTRAIT OF LAURA

One often quoted source of information about Laura is on the flyleaf of Francesco Petrarch's beloved copy of Virgil:

> Laurea, propriis uirtutibus illustris et meis longum celebrata caminibus, primum oculis meis aparatuit sub primum adolescentie mee tempus, anno Domini m° ilj° vij die vj° mensis Aprilis in ecclesia sancte Clare Auin...hora matutina...
> (Laura, illustrious through her own virtues, and long famed through my verses, first appeared to my eyes in my youth, in the year of our Lord 1327, on the sixth day of April, in the church of St. Clare in Avignon, at matins...)[10]
> o

Francesco Petrarch veered between denying his love for Laura and feeling an ironic nostalgia for it. His love for Laura is a private affair, not part of his public persona, which he was so careful to cultivate. Only occasionally do we get an insight into the private Petrarch – outside of the *Rime Sparse*. In his *Letter to Posterity,* he wrote:

> In my younger days I struggled constantly with an overwhelming but pure love-affair, my only one, and I would have struggled with it longer had not premature death, bitter but salutary for me, extinguished the cooling flames.[11]

Francesco Petrarch goes on to say that he does not deny having 'desires of the flesh', but that, after forty, he not only renounced them, but had no recollection of them. This is a bland lie to placate the severe, Augustinian conscience in his psyche. In fact, Petrarch was concerned with 'desires of the flesh' right up until his death – he was editing the *Canzoniere* into 1374, as Ernest Wilkins notes in his *Life of Petrarch* (243).

In his *Secretum,* in reply to another of St Augustine's accusations, Francesco says of his beloved:

> Do you realize that you are referring to a woman whose mind, ignoring earthly cares, burns with celestial desires? In whose aspect,

as truth is truth, shines heavenly beauty? whose behaviour is an example of perfect virtue? whose voice, whose eyes, are more than mortal, whose very walk seems no human action?[12]

What did this Goddess, who walked in beauty, look like? We find she was an angelic figure just like the angels of the *dolce stil novo*:

I wish to praise my lady truly and compare the rose and the lily to her; more than the morning star does she shine and appear.

apostrophizes Guido Guinlcelli, and goes on with all the usual comparisons.

Throughout the *Rime Sparse*, Francesco Petrarch does the same: one of his trademarks, as with Dante Alighieri, is to go over the top with the superlatives, to drown the reader in a luxurious flood of delicious words. This in itself is erotic, but coupled with the psychic pressure being brought to bear upon sexual desires and upon a sensual being, the beloved, the result is often overwhelming erotic.

All courtly love is erotic – in its choice of words, in its way of describing the beloved, in its relationship with the beloved, in its ecstasies and despairs, in its opulent rhetoric and in its aims of entertaining and pleasing an audience.

Francesco Petrarch sexualizes Laura in his poesie primarily by describing her eyes in sensual, religious and ecstatic terms. Like the troubadours and the *stil novisti*, the *Minnesängers* and the Sicilian poets, Petrarch uses the concept of love attacking the initiate with arrows of desire that pierce through the eyes.

There are more poems to Laura's eyes than to any part of her body or persona in the *Canzoniere*. Laura's eyes are nothing less than the way to Heaven, as one of the great *canzoni*, number 70, explains:

Gentil mia Donna, I'veggio
nel mover de' vostr' occhi un dolce lume
che mi mostra la via ch' al ciel conduce

(My noble Lady, I see in the moving of your eyes a sweet light that shows me the way that leads to Heaven) (7: 1-3)

Laura's eyes are so extraordinary even the sun itself is jealous (156: 6 – 'Ch'an fatto mille volle invidia al Sole'); her eyes are so powerful 'she could burn the Rhine with her eyes' (an image that could be straight out of some 1950s, American, sci-fi B-movie: *Laura! The Demon Who Burns Rivers With Her Eyes*, at your local drive-in from next Friday).

Clearly, Laura is a Goddess, a deity with startling powers. There are times when Francesco Petrarch's poetic self seems to believe in his own polished rhetoric: he almost believes that Laura can really burn up rivers, that she can outshine the sun. For the poet, poetry is magic, an undeniably real magic. That is, the poet invest in her/ his creation: for her/ him, it has (or should have if they are a half decent poet) an authenticity and a truth, a piquancy that also should, ultimately, be fully appre-hensible by anyone who comes into contact with it.

Laura's eyes kill. Love assails the poet with the full force of death. Her eyes consume the poet and destroy him (72: 37-39). The first time he sees her, and the times afterwards, are fatal moments, for they involve not only the vision of her beauty, but also the realization that such a revelation of The Beautiful brings with it death – not only the death of being consumed by love, but also the death of the image of loveliness which the poet beholds.

From the beginning, the *Rime Sparse* is death-aware. The tears are flowing even in sonnet number three. Love strikes a mortal blow. Love is often called a battle, and is described by men in the terms of chivalrous war, and when Love's arrow strikes it is no exception: the poet is mortally wounded. The very act is not only erotic, in its fusion of love and death (or in this case, sex and pain), it is also heroic.

To be 'mortally wounded' by Love makes the lover some-thing of a warrior. It seems the poet can do no wrong, because every aspect of his gigantic construction seems to place him in a flattering light. His poetry is brilliant, his philosophy is solid, his humility, loyalty and servitude all win him points, as does his acute sense of suffering. If ever there was a work of art that aims at self-glorification, this is it.

SIX

❧

LOVE IN THE *RIME SPARSE*

veggio, penso, ardo, piango; et chi mi sface
sempre m' è inanzi per mia dolce pena:
guerra è 'l mio stato, d'ira e di duol piena,
et sol di lei pensando o qualche pace.
(I am awake, I think, I burn, I weep; and she who destroys me is
always before me, to my sweet pain: war is my state, full of sorrow
and suffering, and only thinking of her do I have any peace.)

Francesco Petrarch, *Rime Sparse* (sonnet 164: 5-8)

THE FIRE OF LOVE

The look of Laura burns, kills, consumes, destroys. The many,
many references to Laura's eyes emphasize firstly the light in
them – this is the light of religious revelation. For the first time,
the initiate, the would-be lover *sees*. His 'doors of perception', as
William Blake would put it, have been cleansed. With renewed
vision, the world seems transformed. Hence the Look is mystical,
and the religious dimension of it is stressed by most love poets,
and especially by the troubadours, the *dolce stil novo* poets, and by
Dante Alighieri and Francesco Petrarch. All those allusions to the

eyes of Laura (on pages 38, 44, 46, 62, 164, 174, 214, 270, 290, 302, 316, 356 and 370, for example), emphasize not only the light of revelation, but also the fire of love.

The poetic connections between fire, passion, sex and love are reflected in the use of symbols and images everywhere in Western poetry, which speak of hearts, suns, roses, blood, flames and the colours gold and red. All of this imagery can be reduced to one word: *passion*. The word so neatly combines Christian Passion with personal suffering, desire for sex and desire for transcendence.

Francesco Petrarch is no exception when it comes to using the archetypal, even stereotypical symbolism and imagery of poetry. The poet cuts his hand on the thorns of the Rose of Love just as Sleeping Beauty pricks her finger on the spinning wheel of life. When blood is shed, the myth becomes real.

When blood is shed, things start to happen. With the revelation, the transformations begin: in the work of Francesco Petrarch, as in Dante Alighieri's art, the Look of the beloved is an erotic death which inaugurates an era for the poet of continuous pain lightened only very infrequently by the beloved.

It is all done with vision, with looks. There are so few dialogues in the *Rime Sparse*, as in the *Vita Nuova*. There is much interiorized speech and debate, but hardly any conversations between the poet and the beloved. Instead, the poet muses on the same colours, again and again: red, white and gold.

Thus in sonnet 157 of the *Rime Sparse* we read of Laura as a Goddess with hair like gold, a face of 'warm snow', ebony eyebrows and eyes like stars. The phoenix of sonnet 185 wears a scarlet dress 'with a cerulean border sprinkled with roses'; naturally she has a white neck. In *canzone* 323, when Laura is more clearly an angel, we see her in a garment 'so woven that it appeared gold and snow together'. The colours are those of the mediæval era but made even more glowing, even more fiery. The colours introduce one of the main effects of the erotic look of the beloved: the burning pain of love.

BURNING LOVE

Burning from cold – this is a typical Petrarchan conceit, a literary style that has been done to death since the *Rime Sparse* started to circulate about the world. The key element of the Petrarchan conceit is to bring together opposites, the hot and the cold, the fiery and flamy and the wintry and snowy.

The literary conceits echo the dichotomy that is always present in Francesco Petrarch's poetic cycle – between Heaven and Earth, between fear and desire, between sexuality and spirituality, between distance and nearness, between yearning and disgust, between memory and hope for the future. Petrarch never is satisfied. He runs from one side to the other, from wall to wall, between the sets of opposites he creates to form the moral and emotional structure of his poetic world.

Like the Sufi mystic who wishes to burn and dissolve in Allah as the moth wants to frazzle in the flame of a candle, the poet aches to be dissolved in the beloved. As Francesco Petrarch says in the *Rime*'s sonnet 19: 'I know well I am pursuing what burns me'. The poet goes towards Love as the soldier goes into a hopeless battle – knowing he will die. But the glory is all his. Or so he thinks. Thus runs the reasoning of the chivalrous lover of the Middle Ages.

In Francesco Petrarch's poetry, as in all love poets, the hotter the fire of love is, the richer the spiritual apotheosis. As the Sufi poet-mystic Jalal al-Din Rumi said: 'It is the flame of Love that fired me',[1] while al-Nuri said: 'the ecstasy with which I burn/ Sears out my thoughts',[2] and in the Christian religion, mystics of all kinds use fire to describe love: the typical scenario is that of the lonely mystic swallowed up in darkness, yearning for God's touch and receiving it as a mystical immolation. St John of the Cross says that initiates 'burn sweetly in God,'[3] while Jan van Ruysbroeck describes his spiritual union of the soul with God in distinctly nuptial terms: the mystic fire 'makes the lovers melt into each other.'[4] Ruysbroeck is talking of the holiest of holies, but in explicitly erotic terms. He could easily be describing the sex act.

Francesco Petrarch, like the mystics, is 'afire with love',[5] and the mystical fire of love rages throughout the *Rime Sparse*. In *ballata* 52, he relates that 'she made me, even now when the sky is burning, all tremble with a chill of love'; in sonnet 32 the poet says, 'I shiver in mid-summer, burn in winter'; and in sonnet 133 he writes:

> Thoughts of you are arrows, your face a sun
> and with all these weapons Love pierces me. (133: 9-11)

Troubadour poetry abounds in descriptions of the flames of love, of sparks igniting the fire of love in the hearts of trembling poets. Francesco Petrarch takes all those courtly conceits and exaggerates them, puts them into finely-turned sonnets, so that they seem fresh, even though, in the *Canzoniere*, they are already tired, old and decadent. The *Canzoniere* is both the apotheosis and the death of courtly love poetry, much as the Virgin Mary died, mortally, yet ascended to Heaven.

Like the phoenix, the Petrarch-poet dies in the fire of love, only to be reborn through the pain of love. Any thought, word or look of the lady feeds his fiery love, as he says in sonnet 175. The problem is, as he explains in sonnet 182, that love heats up the lover's heart one minute, and the next freezes it. If love is hot, the lady is cold, too cold, as in poem 202. And so the metaphors run on and on. The same basic antagonisms and oppositions are repeated, but in slightly different guises: the sky is hot then cold; it is Winter then Summer; fire then ice assaults the body; in *canzone* 207 the poet is wax and the 'angelic sparks' (Laura's eyes) melt him.

The Petrarchan states pivot around *fiama* (flame), *foco* (fire), *geio* (freezing) and *ghiaccio* (ice): the poetic effect is a vertiginous whirling through a rainbow of emotions from utter despair to bright elation.

Francesco Petrarch's is a poetry of extremes. There is no middle state of indifference. The Petrarch-poet is either up or down, ecstatic or melancholy. Laura's eyes, likened to a spring, a phoenix, a treasure, an angel, the sun, or a star, haunt him and torment him, yet the poet manages to transcend her, her torture, his despair and the vicissitudes of life. How? Through poetry, through the act of making poetry, which in turn re-makes life. (But not completely: there is always something incomplete in the art of Petrarch, something not quite fully achieved or fully transformed, something held back, something ironic, something too self-conscious, too easily, slickly produced. Petrarch is certainly slick: he knows how to create a superb surface sheen to his poems, as the Renaissance painters such as Andrea Sarto and Raphael Sanzio knew how to give their pictures a richness that can dazzle.)

PORTRAIT OF FRANCESCO PETRARCH

Petrarch identified himself at various times as a poet, a historian, a rhetorician, and amoral philosopher.

Charles Trinkaus, *The Poet as Philosopher* (1)

Francesco Petrarch was the most remarkable man of his time; and he is one of the most remarkable men of all time.

Ernest Hatch Wilkins, *Life of Petrarch* (v)

Francesco Petrarch is the Renaissance artist who absorbed the teaching and art of the Classical world and applied to his own art. He was acutely aware of the past. Many ghosts and ancestors of earlier years haunt him. The past was clearly alive for him. He wrote letters to his heroes: Cicero, Horace, Virgil, Homer, Livy, Seneca and Quintilian. His beloved writers – Virgil, Cicero and

Augustine – appear again and again in his works: if not in a direct reference, then in an allusion. Petrarch is one of the most well-read, most educated of all poets – and certainly of the poets of his time. For Petrarch, culture was a living thing with which he communicated; for him, books were not merely objects, they were personalities and friends.6 Petrarch related to books the way people today relate to characters in soap operas or movies, or the way paintings in a much-visited museum can seem like old friends. In a letter of 1346, Petrarch wrote:

> Books have indeed a special fascination. Books delight us through and through, they converse with us, they give us good advice, they become living companions to us.7

He was very hungry – for culture, for philosophy, for ideas and views. The pleasure of reading is primary in Francesco Petrarch's œuvre, as it is in the work of modern authors such as John Cowper Powys, Henry Miller, and Marcel Proust.

Francesco Petrarch must have felt himself to be in a kind of cultural isolation in his retreat in the Vaucluse in Southern France. Books, then, would have been a lifeline to refined thought. As Arthur Rimbaud spoke of being hungry for books in Charleville in Northern France before he went to Paris in the late 19th century, so Petrarch in Provence 600 years earlier felt the need to keep in touch with city life, with the manners and morals of urban culture.

Thus he was, like Rainer Maria Rilke, D.H. Lawrence and André Gide, an obsessive letter writer, and in this way he kept abreast of the latest developments in society. If he had lived in the 21st century, he might have led one life as a retiring scholar in some leafy university town (Oxford or Princeton perhaps), but he would have been a 'news junkie' – a secondary, inner life – listening continually to the radio, and lapping up TV news, surfing the internet, and keeping in touch with many people all the time on his cel phone.

One is struck by the number of places that Francesco Petrarch visited or lived in – the key cities of the mediæval era: Rome, Avignon, Venice, Pisa, Paris, Florence, Ghent, Cologne, Montpellier, and Arezzo. He was a well-travelled man. His self-crowning in Rome too is astonishing, partly because he had achieved so little in poetry at the time.[8]

According to Ernest Wilkins (17), Francesco Petrarch was impressive, widely travelled, uniquely gifted, friendly, highly intelligent, well-informed and an easy talker. The range of his acquaintances is certainly impressive – few poets in history have been so well connected.

Francesco Petrarch loved the Vaucluse, loved returning there – so he could work on his studies, and sink back into nature. His experience of the Vaucluse informs much of the *Rime Sparse* (in its nature mysticism, for instance). He hated city life, and lived frugally (but enjoyed social contact). He dreamt of uniting Italy politically (see his famous 'Italiania' poem in the *Canzoniere*). He veered emotionally from pole to pole. At times, in depression, he would write of his 'hatred and contempt for the human state' (*Letter To Posterity*).[9]

Ernest Wilkins claims in his life of Francesco Petrarch that the dominant trait in Petrarch's nature was a constant desire 'to love and to be loved' (251). It was, rather, a desire to make contact, to be taken seriously, to be seen to be making a significant contribution to culture, to poetry, to history. One might see Petrarch's lust for poetic fame and his love of Laura to be wholly separate – the public and private personas. But in fact Petrarch fused them together at every opportunity in the *Canzoniere*: Laura is not to be split apart from the poetic, Imperial laurel.

One of the more intriguing of Francesco Petrarch's friendship was with the great Italian painter Simone Martini, one of the absolute masters of Renaissance art. Martini's *Annunciation* (Uffizi Gallery, Florence)[10] is one of the most accomplished depictions of the holy meeting of the Handmaid of the Lord with his angelic messenger. It is a painting of swooning emotion – the Virgin bends away from the inrushing archangel like a flower in the wind. The *Ave Maria* streamers run from Gabriel's mouth to the Madonna's mouth. The gestures are full of fluid movement. As art critic Bruce Cole writes in *Siennese Painting*, Martini's *Annunciation* is

> a very sumptuous painting. Gold is everywhere: on the throne, in the angel's robe and wings and hem, on the haloes, in the background.[11]

Gold is used profusely in early Renaissance, Siennese art, as is a particular sepia hue to the skin. All of Simone Martini's works – the *Mæsta*, the *Madonna of Humility* and the St Martin fresco cycle in Assisi – reveal a sensitive touch, especially in the faces and gestures, and Martini's art is the height of the Early Renaissance, as much as Giotto, Masaccio or Fra Angelico. Interestingly, a Giotto *Madonna* was the only painting that Petrarch owned.[12]

The painting that Simone Martini did for Francesco Petrarch's copy of Virgil is in the Ambrosian Library in Milan. The portrait of Laura that Petrarch commissioned Martini to make has been lost. This is a sad loss, for the portrait was clearly extraordinary. As Petrarch states in sonnet 77 of the *Rime Sparse*: 'The work is one of those which can be imagined only in Heaven, not here among us' (9-10).

Of course, it would have been a face painted in the Siennese style, with that sallow, brown skin, slightly slitted eyes and elongated features. I for one would love to see Simone Martini's portrait of Laura de Sade. And if you had to chose any artist of the era to paint her, Simone Martini would be in the top three of the list. For creating a feeling of sweetness and tenderness, along with a delicate but assured graphic line, Martini has few equals.

And in the art of Sandro Botticelli, Dante Alighieri's *Divine Comedy* found an ideal illustrator (therre have been many): Botticelli's faint, pencil drawings of the interlocking circles of Dante's cosmos are superbly realized. Like Gustave Doré, Botticelli shows us the full splendour of Dante's Paradise. Simone

Martini, likewise, is the right choice to depict Petrarch's poetic world.

THE STORY OF LOVE

> Mille trecento ventisette, a punto
> su l'ora prima, il di sesto d'aprile,
> nel laberinto intrai, ne veggio ond' esca.
> (One thousand three hundred twenty seven, exactly at the first hour of
> the sixth day of April, I entered the labyrinth, nor do I see where I
> may get out of it.)
>
> Francesco Petrarch, *Canzoniere* (sonnet 211, 12-14)

The maze of love is all of Francesco Petrarch's own making. Though the courtly love poets and others after them blamed 'Love' or Cupid for firing his arrows at them, love is an entirely human-made affair. God or Venus or whoever has nothing to do with it. God only encourages divine love – that is, love of God.

The 'story' outlined in Francesco Petrarch's *Canzoniere* begins on April 6, 1327, as poem 211, above, notes.
- Laura teases him (poems 45, 46, 87);
- she falls ill (between poems 30 and 50, and 133-7);
- she recovers (33-34);
- Simone Martini paints her (77-78);
- the poet frees himself, then lapses (55);
- Laura is in love, perhaps (88);
- there are separations (41-43);
- Petrarch visits Italy (129, 180);
- he returns via the River Rhône (208);
- he prays for release (62 – this is in 1338);
- Laura leaves a glove at Petrarch's house (199-201);
- she is offended by a remark of his (206);

- she sails on the Rhône (225);
- she is kissed by an important visitor (238);
- an old man compliments the lovers (243);
- they grow old (168, and also 12, 90, 127);
- they have eye infections (231/3);
- Laura is sick (248-255);
- she dies (267-8);
- the poet's released from passion (270);
- he has another lover (271);
- the year 1358 marks the end of the affair (364);
- pleas to God occur in 365;
- and to the Virgin in 366.

We know far less about the actual circumstances of Laura and Francesco Petrarch's romance than the background to William Shakespeare's *Sonnets* (and that is very sketchy). The erotic triangle of Shakespeare's *Sonnets* endlessly fascinates critics, who debate the hints at biography in the poems and offer up different personages to represent the Dark Lady and the Friend.

In Francesco Petrarch's poem cycle, a key mystery is the exact identity of Laura, but there are numerous aspects of their romance which we don't know about (such as, what was their love affair really like? How long did it last? Who else knew about it? and so on). However, it shouldn't really matter: we must get beyond the biographical level and look at the works.

The sequence of events in the *Rime Sparse* is emotional, and follows the trajectory of a typical love affair: he sees her; falls in love; creates myths around her; imagines meeting her in several situations; imagines her as a Goddess, etc; he celebrates anniversaries; she dies; he mourns; he is beset by regrets, bitterness, fantasies; he renounces her and earthly love and finds solace/salvation in the Virgin Mary.

The story, as such, is essentially one of desire. Francesco Petrarch veers between desiring Laura and desiring total transcendence of fleshly love. The Petrarch-poet is never satisfied: this is one of the hallmarks of the artist. Nothing is quite good enough, passionate enough, rich enough. There must always be Something More Than This.

In Francesco Petrarch's literary output, we find a restlessness that is eternal, and is one of the aspects of his poetic personality that renders him so fresh. He wrote in 1336 to Giacomo Colonna:

> My wishes fluctuate and my desires conflict, and in their conflict they tear me apart. Thus does the outer man struggle with the inner.[13]

LOVE AS PAIN

Love is pain, suffering, death, sin, vice, fornication and the source of all ills, according to Christianity. Human, erotic love, that is. Love of God is holy, while love within marriage is grudgingly sanctified. But the kind of love Francesco Petrarch has for Laura de Sade is condemned. Why? Because it veils the yearning soul from God. God hates this kind of love because He is not involved with it. Human love excludes God, and He gets lonely, poor thing.

Thus mystics, though they speak of the divine in erotic, human terms, always emphasize that one must get beyond human love. The Catholic mystics were marked by their lack of relations with others – they lived ascetic, monastic, celibate, chaste lives.

In his scholastic retreat in the Vaucluse in South France, Francesco Petrarch might have intended to while away his life in scholarly pursuits. But love invests him with maximum desire, and he succumbs.

In exalting the suffering of love, Francesco Petrarch turns loving into martyrdom, and makes himself a holy martyr, someone who dies daily for Love (God). Every day the poet writhes in love-pain, and the deeper the despair and the more fervent the torment, the more beatific and celebrated his apotheosis. Petrarch's apotheosis, when he is canonized and beatified, is as much poetic as religious. That is, he desires a poetic transcendence where he is applauded by other poets, by readers and critics. His salvation will be jointly poetic and religious. The Christian saints, fathers, theologians and mystics that dwell in Dante Alighieri's Paradise are there partly because they are artists, not just because they are holy. Art is revered in the works of Dante and Petrarch. Thus Petrarch will ascend to Heaven, he hopes, not simply because of his faith, but because he is (he knows) a great poet.[14]

The poems of the first part of the *Canzoniere*, before Laura's death, are more erotic, passionate and extreme in their depiction of fear and desire. In the second part, the poems become more refined, as the poet yearns for transcendence from this Earth to join Laura in Heaven. In the second part, the Petrarchan poet regrets much of his former loving: here the sublimation begins, the movement from earthly to divine desires.

At times, Francesco Petrarch is as clichéd and repetitive as a banal pop song, as in *canzone* 71 where he says:

At your appearance anguish and pain flee,
and at your departure they return together.

But it is true, and needs to be said (but Petrarch also invented or re-invented many of the banalities of love and desire that crop up in modern pop music). The Arabic poets have a succinct way of putting this anguish of proximity and distance:

She looks,
the arrow penetrates.
She turns,
the arrow is pulled out.
(Al-Ahnaf)[15]

When Laura appears, pain dissolves, even when her appearance is that of a ghost, or in a dream, or a reverie: the poet can, in fact, 'wish up' Laura just as the fairy tale character can wish things up with their magic pots and treasure boxes. Like Aladdin with his lamp in *1001 Nights*, the poet can conjure up personages. In sonnet 111 Laura appears, but not in the flesh: she materializes while the poet 'was sitting alone with lovely thoughts of love' (111: 1-4). Poetry is magic, and the poet is the archaic shaman, the magician ('poet' in Greek – *poetas* – means 'maker').

To those not in love, to non-artists, this magic can seem like self-deception. On one level of course this is what it is. But the poet is happy with her/ his self-deception. As Francesco Petrarch says in *canzone* 129:

> I feel Love so close that my soul is satisfied by its own deception. (36-37)

The artist believes in her/ his own creation. S/he must do, for it to have any valuable effect. For the artist, art is real as life is real.

The great Islamic mystic Abu Hamid Muhammad ibn Muhammad al-Ghazzali said: 'I love the Real', meaning Allah;[16] it is the same for the artist. Francesco Petrarch believed in his poetic powers. He feeds off them as he feeds off love. In sonnet 134 of the *Rime Sparse* he goes through the usual sufferings of love:

> I find no peace, and I am not at war,
> I fear and hope, and burn and I am ice;
> I fly above the heavens, and lie on earth
> and I grasp nothing and embrace the world. (1-4)

But he ends the sonnet by saying: 'I thrive on pain and laugh with all my tears'.[17] Pain makes poetry, in short: from pain comes poetry.

The pain, the restlessness, the dissatisfaction, the agony of it all – this is what powers the poetry. This is not to say art must come out of agony, as in the work of Vincent van Gogh or Egon Schiele, where the artist is a hero who must suffer terribly for art. No: but in love poetry, pain is nearly always uppermost.

Francesco Petrarch's aim, like that of so many love poets, is to make pain pleasure: or if not to make pain pleasurable, at least to make the wallowing in it pleasurable. As he writes in sonnet 226: '[t]o weep always is my highest delight, laughing is pain. (5-6).

The masochism in courtly love culture is developed into the most refined art in Francesco Petrarch's *Canzoniere*. So many of his sonnets celebrate the pain of love – and the ecstasy of it. In sonnet 236, the poet claims love is a transgression: he teeters on the brink of collapse. Like many lovers, the poet treads a tightrope, a knife edge, on one side is the chaos of despair, on the other is shame, sin, regret and self-loathing. Ahead of him stands his beloved. He has to keep reaching for her, knowing all the while they will never quite meet. There will always be some distance between them. But the poet trudges onward:

I have never been weary of loving you,
my Lady, nor shall I be while I live... (1-2)

The pain of loving a Goddess is luscious, and flatters the poet's (and the reader's) notions of idealism, loyalty, suffering and dignity (and artistry as a poet, and intelligence as a reader). So the poet says

though she kills me a thousand times a day,
I shall still love her and hope in her (172: 12-13)

In a thousand different ways, Francesco Petrarch poeticizes this child-like dependency on the beloved woman. In sonnet 267 of the *Canzoniere*, the Goddess becomes not only the food but the air which the poet must have to be able to breathe. He says 'for you I must burn, in you breathe' (267: 9). Because love is painful, then life itself must be painful for the lover and the love poet. The two – love and life – are the same thing. If love is horrible, then life must be horrible; conversely, if love is wonderful, then life must be wonderful. For love takes over the poet and the lover completely.

So Arnaut Daniel, fêted by Dante Alighieri and Francesco Petrarch, says: 'her heart submerges mine utterly'.[18] Castelloza, a female troubadour (born *c.* 1200) wrote:

> every Joy is meaningless to me
> but yours.[19]

The love poet expects everything of her/ his beloved, even the restoration of the world. Love is capable of anything, the lover and the love poet reckon. If the lover is happy, s/he looks outside and – *lo and behold, by the gods!* – the sun is shining. If the lover is melancholy, s/he looks outside and – *lo and behold!* – it is raining.

These banal attitudes, rehashed today in pop promos, in advertizing, in Hollywood movies, in a billion television and web commercials, have a magical aspect: people in the West really do believe that love is a transforming power. Love really does transform the world, Westerners think. Not just in Christianity is this true, but in much of Western art. So when Francesco Petrarch moans in poem 312: '[l]iving is such heavy and long pain' (12), he means he is out of love, has not seen the beloved for ages, or is not with her (if he was with her, he wouldn't be writing poetry!).

The real meaning of such lines in Francesco Petrarch's work and in all love poets' writings is that when one is out of love, wallowing in love-pain, life itself is hideous. Love poets narrow their focus down so much they place all their emphasis on love. They expect love is do everything, to transform their lives. Expecting so much from love, they can only be disappointed. They are asking too much of love, of their beloved, of the experience.

FROM PAIN TO POETRY

The method is simple: life flows into art, and art enhances life. The poet falls in love; s/he falls out of love. Pain follows. From pain comes art. Art in turn nurtures life, makes life easier to bear. This is not idealism, this is precisely what art does. Art not only helps to form a concept of self, of identity (a very postmodern function), it also nurtures life, enables rebirth.

Francesco Petrarch has this view of a magical, transformative poetics. A number of times he states that the act of writing poetry helps to bear the pain of love. The act of speaking alleviates the pain ('I seek to lighten my pain by speaking' [270: 4]). Why does he write poetry, why does he sing? – 'because, singing, pain becomes less bitter' (23: 4).

But poetry is more than a drug to numb the pain of love. It is therapy, transformation, magic, a methodology, a life support system. By speaking, the poet lets all the pain flow away. In theory. The problem with Francesco Petrarch, as with other love poets from Catullus in ancient times to Elizabeth Bishop in the modern era, is that by speaking and writing poetry about love, one enhances the pain. Self-deception becomes self-torture. The act of making poetry rehearses the pain, goes over it again and again, making it worse. And Petrarch loves this. He loves going over old wounds and opening them up, rubbing salt into them, making them re-bleed:

by speaking I renew the burning desire. (37: 49-50)

In the later poems, the Petrarchan poet tires of the self-deception, the magic, the therapy, the whole poetic process by which life can be renewed. In the *Rime*'s poem 332, the Petrarch-poet claims that there is no art powerful enough to transmit his agony, that poetry no longer offers its former consolations:

my heavy sighs cannot go into rhymes,
and my harsh torment surpasses every style. (11-12)

Wretched, the poet seems condemned to haunt the grave of his love – both Laura's grave and Love's grave, and the grave of his desire. Desire kills, but it murders more than the poet's hopes. The story of the *Rime Sparse* is a 'spiritual autobiography' (to use Robert Graves' phrase for his own love poetry). In the *Canzoniere,* Petrarch shows how 'wretched and happy, day by day, hour by hour. Love has gnawed at me.' (356: 7-8)

Like so many love poets, Francesco Petrarch believes that the pain of love valorizes life, makes it real, authentic, gives it (poetic) weight. Joseph Campbell explains it thus in *The Power of Myth*:

> Love is the burning point of life, and since all life is sorrowful, — so is love. The stronger the love, the more the pain. Love itself is a pain, you might say – the pain of being truly alive. (205)

Ah yes, the poet cries, *at least I am alive if I am feeling this agony of love!* Such an Existential view is one that masculine culture more than feminine culture endorses.

With this fusion of love and pain as a recipe for life we are back with patriarchal notions of love. 'I believe eroticism to be the approval of life, up until death', stated cult French author Géorges Batallle. This is the view of the Surrealist artists with their *amour fou*, of the Marquis de Sade, Charles Baudelaire, Henry Miller, Sigmund Freud, and Jean-Paul Sartre. For male artists, death and pain make life holy. As, D.H. Lawrence said (in *Fantasia of the Unconscious*): '[d]eath is the only pure, beautiful conclusion of a great passion.'[20] Death thus crowns life for the male/ masculine artist – thus the passions of Romanticism end in death (in Johann Wolfgang von Goethe's *Werther*), and Christianity is built on death. Christianity focuses not on the Risen Christ, as it might well do, but on the dying God on the Cross. As in Buddhism, life is seen as suffering.

Elizabeth Browning wrote: 'Not Death, but Love', but male artists focus on death. Their point is that transcendence occurs in death. Through death, one achieves Heaven. Thus Francesco Petrarch all through the *Rime Sparse* yearns to meet Laura in

Heaven, to sit with her at the feet of God.

In the poetry of Dante Alighieri, we find the same desire for transcendence, the same hope for a paradisal re-integration with the beloved. Francesco Petrarch goes to his death, then, with his head hung low in humility, as he hopes to be reunited with his beloved in Heaven. It is the same with Christ on the Cross, crying out to his Father. The poet yearns to be re-united with the Great Mother, the Goddess.

Francesco Petrarch makes this connection between Laura and the Blessed Virgin when he switches from Laura to the Madonna in the final poem of the *Canzoniere*. If Laura does not have the Godly power to draw the poet up to Heaven towards her, perhaps he can beg the Virgin Mary to help him achieve his life-long goal.

Poetry, though, does not exist in Heaven, in God, in the Virgin Mary, or in dead people. It is made by and for living people. And at times in the *Canzoniere*, Francesco Petrarch realizes that the only kind of transcendence worth anything is one that occurs here, right here, and right now. In poem 332 the poet invokes the name of the original magician-poet, Orpheus, and wonders if poetry can bring Laura back from the dead:

> Would that I had so sorrowful a style
> that I could win my Laura back from Death
> as Orpheus won his Eurydice without rhymes,
> for then I would be more glad than ever. (332: 49-52)

SEVEN

ào

LOVE AND NOSTALGIA

Io amai sempre, et amo forte ancora,
et son per amar più du giorno in giorno
quel dolce loco ove piangendo torno
spesse fiate quando Amor m'accora…
(I have always and I still love and I shall day by day love even more
that sweet place where weeping I return many times when Love
saddens me)

Francesco Petrarch, sonnet 85 (1-4)

MEMORY

Love feeds on memory, and poetry thrives on nostalgia. Love
poetry comes out of the disparity between what the poet has now
(no love) and what s/he once had (love). Love poetry pivots
around nearness and distance (spatially), and the past and the
present (temporally). Memory keeps feeding the poet (poets can
never forget) with reminiscences which drive the poet to make up
the distance with some word magic.

Love poetry is all about a gap, a gulf, a distance which has to
be bridged. Lovers are not only apart physically, but also

temporally. Poetry thus becomes an act of magic, whereby the poet aims to bring the beloved back from the past, to resurrect her/ him by means of poetic alchemy, so that they can enjoy each other again. Love poetry conjures up the beloved and the experience of her/ him. The love poet resuscitates the beloved, the experience, the desire, the memory. The love poet knows well that it is an impossible task, that only gods can bring people back from the dead. Yet the beloved must come back bodily, for human love centres on physicality.

Love poetry is thus an art of presence and absence. Love poetry is always written alone, when the lover has been gone for a moment, an hour, a week, or years. Love poetry hopes to bridge the gulf, to travel, in occult fashion, towards the beloved. It is impossible, but the love poet persists in trying. Doomed to failure, the love poet is a special kind of artist, an artist of nostalgia.

Her/ his act is a rebellion against the violence and ambiguity of the human condition. The love poet aches for a world in which love can rule supreme, but knows, in her/ his rational, day-to-day consciousness, that this can never occur.

The love poet tortures her/ himself, time after time. Desire keeps nagging away, and the poet responds with ever more ambitious works. To celebrate the lack is the love poet's aim, and we find this in all kinds of love poetry, from Greek epigrams to the latest popular songs: *you were here, and now you're not, and I weep* is the fundamental message. There might be Christian overtones – the poet might confuse his human beloved with the Almighty Beloved, but the lack and the desire stems not from the lonely soul being separated from God, but from the physical/ psychological distance between one body and another, between one desire and another.

All this desire and self-torture and nostalgia is summarized fervently by Francesco Petrarch in the *Canzoniere* in his sonnet 273, where he berates himself for keeping on with the self-deception, the aching, the nostalgia, the burning:

What are you doing? What are you thinking? Why do you still look back to a time that can never return anymore? My comfortless soul, why do you still add fuel to the fire where you are burning?

The gentle words and the sweet glances that you have described and depicted one by one, have been taken from the earth, and it is, you well know, unseasonable and too late to seek them here.

Ah, do not renew what kills us; do not follow any longer a deceptive yearning thought, but a firm and certain one that may guide us to a good end.

Let us seek Heaven, if nothing pleases us here; for we ill saw that beauty if living and dead it was to rob us of peace.

LOVE INTO NOSTALGIA

Most if not all of the great poems about love are written after the event: William Shakespeare's *Sonnets*, Maurice Scève's *Délie*, Dante Alighieri's *Vita Nuova* and the fragments of Sappho. Love poetry is nostalgia: a wallowing in feeling made into art. Among modern poets, C.P. Cavafy is the supreme poet of erotic nostalgia. In Cavafy's poetry, mythology, memory, eroticism and place (Alexandria) fuse. While the nostalgia of poets such as Constantin Cavafy, Paul Verlaine and Francesco Petrarch can seem like pathetic wallowing in emotional self-deception, it stems from a belief in the transformative powers of poetry.

For poetry is like mysticism: it agrees with the Tibetan mystic Jetsun Milarepa (d. 1135) who said: 'think of past, future and present as all one'.[1] This is a radical view, typical of Oriental mysticism. Western poetry and religion is not so rigorous. There is always a little left over of the Western ego in the mystical experience.

Francesco Petrarch's self-aware, self-analytical, self-reflexive poetry threatens to consume itself, to pile self-parody upon self-parody. The memory of the sight of Laura is enough to set him off on this self-destructive journey. Speaking of her beauty, he says 'the very memory seems to consume me' (258: 5; 'che pur il rimembrar par mi consumi'). Why does he keep going over the death of his love? He asks himself this question many times: 'What are you yearning for still?' (264: 20), 'Ah, why do you consume yourself before the time?' (279: 9).

Francesco Petrarch simply could not resolve this problem, this question of love and nostalgia, desire and revulsion, what the Ancient Roman poet Catullus called 'odi et amo' ("I hate and I love").[2] With Petrarch, the problem is a mass of conflicts. His unconscious, the wish-fulfilling element, plays God, and crucifies his ego, his self, which yearns for his *anima*, his soul-image (Laura), while his rational self, his conscience, the super-ego, looks on in bewilderment and tries to step in and avert catastrophe. There is no way out, it seems, of this downslide into self-crucifixion. In the *Epistolæ familiares*, he wrote:

> What I used to love, I love no longer. No, I am lying. I love it still, but more moderately. No, again I have lied. I love, but with more shame, more sadness; and now at least I have told the truth. This is the fact: I love, but I love what I long not to love, what I should like to hate. I love nonetheless, but unwillingly, under compulsion, with sadness and mourning.[3]

We see here how Francesco Petrarch's statements and counter-statements echo the poetic structure of the sonnet. Thesis is followed by antithesis; each statement is modulated by others; the poet is in constant battle with himself. Love comes first, then introspection, then poetry: as Morris Bishop notes in *Petrarch and His World*, the 'rhyme and rhythm impose their obligations, and have that effect on the thought.' (152) When Laura dies, the conflict gets worse if anything, 'it frees his fantasy all the more', as Robert M. Durling comments (*Petrarch's Lyric Poems*, 21).

In the second half of the *Rime Sparse*, Francesco Petrarch imagines Laura's presence in a number of situations. He fantasizes about her, replacing actual absence with poetic presence.

TIME AND NUMBER

For an obsessively nostalgic poet, dates are magical and are celebrated as holy anniversaries. The day that Francesco Petrarch first saw Laura is exalted, just as Dante Alighieri held dear the first time he saw Beatrice in Firenze. The day was when it all began, the love poet muses: the beginning of the ecstasy and the despair. We find in Petrarch's *œuvre* many poems that celebrate special dates, anniversaries and numbers. In this way, Petrarch produces his own version of the seasons, of the cycles of time, of the year, within his own secret numerology.

Francesco Petrarch's mythology of time parallels and expands the Christian calendar. For him, the day Friday is holy: it relates to Good Friday, and also the Sixth Day of Creation (it is also sacred to Venus and the Goddess in traditional symbolism). Friday, like the number six, thus represents for him redemption and the culmination of God's work (completion on the Sixth Day). The number six is magical for Petrarch in the way that three and nine were for Dante Alighieri.

In traditional symbolism, six is equilibrium, union, health, beauty, and the six senses. Six as a symbol is also echoed in Petrarch's poetic forms, particularly the *sestina* form with its cyclical rhymes in six-line stanzas. The number helps to bind up love, religion and art. The number six, like Laura herself, draws to it many poetic allusions, some personal, some mythic, some religious, some occult.

Poets work in intuitive, associative ways: s/he runs freely through a host of associations. The more allusions one can have in a word, the better. Thus the number six relates in Francesco Petrarch's mythopœia to Christ on the Cross, to his poetic self-crucifixion, to Laura, to the place he first met her (Avignon), to God's perfection, to Neoplatonic thought (in Philo, for instance[4]), to his cyclical/ seasonal celebration of his passion, and so on.

In the poetic writing of Francesco Petrarch, time and the passing of time is a major theme, if not *the* major theme: time flows, beauty dies, love dies, transcending the past is imperative, etc. Time and love cannot be separated, and nor can poetry or love. Each poem commemorates some magical moment; each poem aims to create a magic circle which lies outside of time. In wishing his beloved were back with him, the poet also wishes for timelessness. The love poet, like so many artists, looks back on love as a paradisal occurrence, a time which was blissfully outside of time.

In love poetry, the memory is of a timeless bliss, an ecstasy that literally stands outside of time. Timelessness is one of the hallmarks of the mystical experience, and it is a key element in love poetry. The love poet talks of paradise: paradise is not just erotic entanglements, it is embodied in the images of the enclosed garden of love, in that sacred space set apart from the world, the outside, public world of day-to-day chaos, servitude, ambiguity, and death.

The myths of paradise are widespread: each myth speaks of a sacred time, an original timeless time when the sacred displaced the profane and bliss was uppermost.[5] Looking back nostal ogically on the earlier, better, golden days, a common enough sentiment, is bound up also with the experience of childhood. As a child, one supposes, things were easier, simpler and beautiful. Perception was not clouded by deceit, confusion and ambivalence. Childhood was a great time, and the lover similarly looks back on the former romance as a bliss time.

Each love poem, then, aims to recreate that blissful time and space, where one could kiss endlessly and perceptions were clear and exquisite. The composing of the poem rehearses psychologically that sacred moment, takes the poet back there. The poet is a master of disbelief: s/he will unashamedly suspend her/ his cynicism and believe in her recreation of bliss.

This is what Francesco Petrarch does in each poem in the *Rime Sparse*, this is what all love poets do. Whether it is fantasy, fact, biography, memory, dream or lies doesn't matter. What counts is the desire: the intensity, the difficulty, the beauty and the despair of desire.

Sonnet 61 of the *Canzoniere* commemorates the birth of the poet's desire in the clearest fashion: the moment, the hour, the day, the year, is seen as holy:

> Blessed be the day, the month, the year,
> the season and the time, the hour, the instant,
> the gracious countryside, the place where I
> was struck by those two lovely eyes that bound me... (61: 1-4)

Though blessed, the moment of love's birth is also hated: in poem 329, Francesco Petrarch mourns that sacred time in a deliberately over-rapturous fashion:

> O day, O hour, O last moment, O stars sworn to impoverish me. (1-2)

SACRED SPACES

Each place where the beloved walked is sacred; where she sat, under which tree, next to which stream, on which hill. Each place becomes a shrine to lost love, a memorial, a temple. Nature in Francesco Petrarch's poesie is a temple where he goes to worship his desire, his beloved. Like a serial killer who repeatedly haunts the grave of his murder victim, the poet hovers around the places where Laura walked. Returning to the place reactivates the old emotions (and, similarly, certain people can set off the 'tape recordings' of ghosts in certain places. This 'television effect' is a well-known phenomenon in paranormal circles). Like Hamlet, Petrarch communes with Laura's ghost. As with the *dolce stil novo*, the beloved is an angel, and everything she touches is sacred. In poem 112, Petrarch explains how emotion is bound up with place:

> Here I saw her all humble and there haughty, now harsh, now gentle, now cruel, now merciful; now clothed in virtue, now in gaiety, now tame, now disdainful and fierce. Here she sang sweetly and here sat down; here she turned about and here held back her step; here with her lovely eyes she transfixed my heart; here she said a word, here she smiled, here she frowned. (5-13)

Quoting Francesco Petrarch's poetry in English prose destroys so much, but the point here is the way in which Petrarch erects a shrine to each gesture, each thought, each look of the beloved, so that we have a record of every tiny, little thing she does (*oh, isn't she cute, every little thing she does!* cries the poet). In this way, the poet fixes the beloved, psychically, and poetically.

The landscape becomes a mirror, reflecting back the poet's desires. The inner and the outer worlds become one. Despondent, the poet searches in nature for some sign of the beloved. Eventually, lost in the depths of his self-delusion, he begins to see the whole of nature as a gigantic poem to her, to Laura, to the beloved.

So, in one of the great *canzone* – 129 – Francesco Petrarch writes:

> I have many times (now who will believe me?) seen her alive in the clear water and on the green grass and in the trunk of a beech tree; and in a white cloud... (40-44)

This is Francesco Petrarch the daydreamer, seeing romantic shapes in clouds. After Laura's death, Petrarch's projections become wilder: he has no hope of seeing her in the flesh, but his imagination can surely conjure up something. At times, the whole landscape speaks to him of his love, as in sonnet 280, where the waters, breeze, branches, birds, flowers, grass and fish are 'all together begging [him] always to love' (280: 9-11). Wandering in his cherished Vaucluse, beside the River Sorgue, Petrarch in sonnet 301 goes his furthest yet in his nature mysticism: he claims he has seen Laura ascend to Heaven, in an Assumption exactly like that of the Madonna (301: 12-14).

The Assumption of the Virgin Mary has a special place within Christianity: she was the only person, apart from Christ, who ascended bodily to Heaven, so her body could be reunited with her soul. This act demonstrates how the Madonna transcended sin, death and the Fall, and it remains controversial.[6]

Francesco Petrarch does not state that Laura blasphemously ascended bodily to Heaven, but he does keep mentioning her beauty, her eyes and hair and so on, while she resides in Heaven waiting for her 'lovely veil', her body, to join her. Further, Petrarch says she went 'naked' to Heaven: this may mean, in the best Augustinian tradition (i.e., heavily ascetic and austere in the Christian sense), that she was pure, but the emphasis on ascending naked is also erotic. Even when she is in Heaven Petrarch eroticizes Laura, and lusts after her even more fervently than when she was alive.

NATURE IN THE *RIME SPARSE*

Nature appears in the *Rime Sparse* in an idealized fashion – as idealized as the mythical landscapes of painters such as Claude Lorrain or Nicholas Poussin (Francesco Petrarch and Dante Alighieri would be quite at home in the 17th century paintings of Classical fantasies and mythologies of Poussin and Claude).

At the same time, Francesco Petrarch's experience of the natural world is based firmly on the landscape of Provence, of the Vaucluse area. It is a world of secret places, of clear, rushing streams and rocky hills. This bright world is reflected in the many poems in the *Canzoniere* which celebrate nature either directly, or through the persona of – guess who? – Laura. Many of the best passages of nature mysticism occur in the *canzoni* and the *sestinas* – in poems 22, 30, 66, 126, 142, 237, and 323).

Landscapes are symbolic,7 in this kind of art, and in Francesco Petrarch's poetry they are symbolic of Laura and his desire for her. The Goddess of ancient times presides over nature; indeed, the Goddess *is* nature; the Goddess controls time, growth, the seasons, the Moon, agriculture and plants. Thus when the Petrarch-poet goes walking in his Arcadia – the Vaucluse in South France – he encounters his Goddess, Laura, in every leaf, blade of grass, stony valley and gurgling river.

Francesco Petrarch's landscapes lie halfway between the idealized Arcadias of Classical, bucolic art, as in the writings of Theocritus and Virgil, and the post-mediæval landscapes that began to appear behind the holy scenes depicted in Early Renaissance painting. The landscapes of Trecento and Quattrocento painting (Giotto, Masaccio, Lippi, Duccio, Angelico) have an air of sweetness and innocence about them – each tree, shrub, stone and hill is drawn with a childlike attention to detail. Petrarch's sense of nature is similarly inclined to awe and clarity: the pictures he renders in the lyrics are those of a landscape of jewel-like brilliance, such as is found in mediæval illuminated manuscripts, or in the paintings of Giotto and early Fra Angelico.

In poem 126 of the *Rime,* Francesco Petrarch describes in luscious terms the '[c]lear, fresh sweet waters', the flowers and trees where his beloved resides. In sonnet 162 he delineates a bounteous nature of 'slender trees and green unripe leaves, delicate pale violets, shady woods', where Laura walks ('Schietti arboscelli, e verdi frondi acerbe;/ Amorosette e pallide viole', 5-7). The landscapes reflect the poet's mood accurately and acutely. Ultimately, they serve the goals of poetry.

More typical in Francesco Petrarch's *Rime Sparse* is the abstract landscape, one in which symbolism is both mysterious and clear. The *sestinas* in particular feature highly symbolic landscapes: in poem 30 the first line introduces a 'youthful lady under a green laurel'; the poet often escapes into the woods (142), or the loved one goes there (214); sometimes the beloved is personified in magical terms as a mediæval beast: the white doe of sonnet 190, for instance, which the poet has to follow.

One of the most common personifications or equations is that of Laura and the breeze: the word-play fuses the two together: in poems such as *sestina* 239, Francesco Petrarch plays with *aurora, l'aura* and *Laura*. It's easy to see why the breeze plays such a large part in the *Canzoniere*: the poet is alone in the countryside: there are no distracting noises of cars, TVs, radios, phones, trains, planes, helicopters, factories or motorcycles. Instead, there are animals, insects, birds and the wind. The breeze moves the leaves softly: easy for a poet to imagine the wind to be the spirit of Laura – and very easy for such yearning, swooning poetry that Petrarch creates.

In myth and religion the wind is phallic, erotic, the spirit or soul, the Creative Word, the *pneuma* – Francesco Petrarch turns around this masculine symbolism and makes the breeze, *l'aura/ Laura*, into the breath of the Goddess.

Laura as the breeze is a major symbol in the *Rime Sparse* – as prominent as Laura as Daphne. Poems such as 194, 196, 197 and 198 form a group of Laura-and-breeze meditations in which the soft touch of the wind arouses and tantalizes the poet. The eroticism of the breeze is only thinly veiled, like the erotic quality of nature in the troubadours' poetry. And if nature can be luscious, it can also be cruel, as in *sestinas* 22 and 60, where ice, snow, rain and freezing cold assail the wandering poet.

Nature is the mirror that the poet, as Narcissus, stares into: s/he can change the mirror so it reflects anything s/he chooses. Nature is bountiful, but a poet such as Francesco Petrarch, as with Arthur Rimbaud or Robert Herrick, makes it work for him: that is, he transforms nature in his poetry to do the jobs he desires. Dazzled as he is by nature, Petrarch only incorporated it into his poetry for strictly artistic reasons. It is there to play its part in his cosmology of love. In the *De remediis utriusque fortunæ*, he writes:

> so many shows and kinds of things, which by strange and marvell-
> ous means do serve to your delight… so great concord of smells and
> colours and tastes, and sounds rising of contraries, so many living
> creatures in the air, upon the land, and in the sea, serving only to your
> use and created only to do man pleasure.[8]

Nature has one important function in Francesco Petrarch's poetic world: it is the space where the poet encounters his beloved. While Beatrice and Dante dwelt in the city, Petrarch and Laura walk together in the countryside. Whether abstract, ideal-ized, actual or dream-like, Petrarch's landscapes are the setting for the mythical meetings of the poet and his beloved. Away from the city, Petrarch can concentrate wholly on his desire. There are no outside forces to disturb his contemplation, no people on the streets (as in Dante Alighieri's Florence in the *Vita Nuova*), no commentators, no other views except the poet's own (and no authority figures, no parents, no priests, no judges, and no night watchmen).

In his Provençal retreat, Francesco Petrarch allows himself free rein in the highly stylized account of his private life. Yet no matter how private and intimate and autobiographical Petrarch might be in his vernacular lyrics, he shapes them, edits them, selects them and polishes them for public consumption. He wants to reach, like any Hollywood producer (or political demagogue), the largest possible audience. (We know, from his self-crowning in Roma, that Petrarch quite enjoyed public adulation).

EIGHT

🙦

THE MYTHOLOGY OF LOVE

As soon as he had entered the spring-drenched cave,
the naked nymphs just as they were, beat their breasts,
for they had seen a man,
and filled the whole copse
with a sudden screaming and, pouring round Diana
they covered her with their bodies; but the goddess
was taller than them, standing head and shoulders above them all.
There is a colour seen in clouds tinged
from the impact
of the facing sun or of the rosy dawn,
that was the colour in Diana's face when she was seen without her
dress…

Ovid, *Metamorphoses*[1]

CLASSICAL MYTHOLOGY

Ovid (43 B.C. - 17 A.D.) was a massive influence on European art:
his influence can be discerned in the work of Shakespeare,
Shelley, Chaucer, Byron, Valéry, Racine, Ronsard, Rilke, Goethe,
Aristo, Tasso, Dante and, more than most, Petrarch.[2]

It is Ovid's rendition of the ancient myths, as much as the

content and drama of them, that was so influential. Ovid did not make the myths his own: rather his was the version of the myths that poets enjoyed.

Francesco Petrarch makes much use of Classical mythology, of Ancient Roman art, history and culture. He alludes to paganism, to pre-Christian mythology, as he does to the *Bible* (it would be impossible for a major, European poet in mediæval times *not* to refer to the *Bible*).

The narrative models evoked in the *Rime Sparse* include Ovid's *Metamorphoses* and Dante Alighieri's *Vita Nuova.*[3] Ovid and Virgil are as powerful a presence as St Augustine and Dante.

In Ovid's *Metamorphoses*, we find the myths of Apollo and Daphne, where the nymph is pursued by Apollo and calls on her father, the river god Peneus, to help her: he changes her into a laurel tree (*Metamorphoses*, 1.452f). This is probably the main mythic scenario used in the *Rime Sparse*, for it binds up actual, holy words (Laura and laurel) with sexuality, Classical mythology, poetry and the necessity of transcendence.

Francesco Petrarch also employs the myth of Narcissus and Echo, which is so pertinent to the artist's fate, and especially that of a love poet: the myth ends with Echo wasting away until she is just a voice, while Narcissus decays into self-love. Petrarch is not only Narcissus, the epitome of the artist, and the religionist, he is Echo, too. Echo's reduction to a voice (*Metamorphoses* 3.339-510) is Beckettian: so many Samuel Beckett anti-heroes are just voices, speaking to themselves in the darkness. And this is precisely the lot of the poet, especially the love-lorn soul. As with the myth of Daphne and Apollo, the myth of Echo and Narcissus is made to express the poetic problem of how, if at all, art can transform life. Petrarch asks the question: how far do his poetic powers stretch, how much magic is there in *Canzoniere*?

Another important ancient myth which is intensely poetic is that of Orpheus and Eurydice. More than Apollo, Orpheus is the god of poetry: he is a shaman, a master of animals who has the magic of music and singing. The poet going into the Underworld to rescue Eurydice is a metaphor or expression of the poetic method, the poetic desire: to achieve the unachievable, to bring back the beloved from the dead, from afar (as all courtly love poets try to do, as Petrarch tries to do in the second half of the *Rime Sparse*).

Poetry aims to resurrect life, to give life renewed vigour, as Orpheus tries to renew the connection with Eurydice. Orpheus' fate is to wander alone, conspiring to conjure ever more beautiful and ambitious lyrics, in order to revivify the world, and his beloved. Orpheus is thus the archetypal lyrical poet, embodying so fully the poetic principles of shamanic magic, supreme desire, ontological restlessness, societal rebellion and alienation, and pure lyricism.

Though he espouses the ethics of the Apollonian poet and scholar, Francesco Petrarch is more typically an Orphic poet, and especially in the *Canzoniere*, which is one long poem of wish-fulfilment: the desire to bring back his beloved Laura from the dead, and, with her, his love of the experience of love.

MYTHOLOGY IN THE *RIME SPARSE*

Mythic love reflects earthly love: the deeds of the deities mirror those of ordinary people – or vice versa. The gods feed off people more than people feed off the gods. Ancient Greek gods and goddesses are approachable, even homely – they are not distant and other-worldly, like Jehovah or God or Allah of monotheism. The Greek gods and goddesses are playful, silly, wrathful, ignorant, deceitful, wily, poetic, difficult, sexy – while the Judæo-Christian God is distant, abstract and rather dull. The Ancient Greek pantheon of gods and goddesses is like the Hindu pantheon: full of life, full of human frailties and desires. The God of Western monotheism takes all the fun out of being a divinity. While the gods of primitive mythology and Classical legends make mistakes, the Judæo-Christian God cannot possibly make a mistake. His subjects make all the errors. God's world is perfect, though he allows the Fall to occur. There are so many flaws in God's plan – it would be obscenely, blasphemously wrong to the Greek gods, and to the people who worshipped them.

Francesco Petrarch veers between the pagan and the Christian, the Classical and the Catholic: he uses Ancient Greek mythology to enlarge upon his theme of erotic love, while Christianity looms above him, quashing eroticism and substituting divine love for earthly desires. But where the Petrarch-poet lives – in the woods, by the rivers, amid the grasses and flowers of Earth – this is where human love takes place, and the natural accompaniment to such erotic love is Greek mythology, not otherworldly, Christian severity.

Francesco Petrarch's Hellenism, then, is associated with the pastoral ethic, with Arcadian idylls, with nature, with eroticism and the beloved; his Catholicism frowns on all such pagan behaviour, and tries to lead him away from it. Petrarch never resolves his conflict: he would like Heaven to be a Garden of Love in the mediæval manner, rather than an abstract, light-filled space out of the *Divina Commedia*.

Examples of Francesco Petrarch's Arcadian mythos include: in *canzone* 129, Petrarch's Laura is compared to Leda's daughter, Helen of Troy: the allusion not only indicates Laura's astonishing beauty, but also the eroticism of Leda's union with Zeus/ Jupiter in the form of a swan; women in love poetry were sometimes compared to swans, as was the Virgin Mary. The swan combines eroticism and death, for it is famous for its death song, the swansong, which is also the poet's song. There is a Christian gloss, too: the swan denotes martyrdom and resignation.[4] Petrarch alludes to all these symbolisms by mentioning Leda rather than Helen of Troy.

In sonnet 167, he alludes to 'a heavenly siren' ('del ciel

sirena') – Francesco Petrarch was ever haunted by sirens, who are essentially the Goddess in her cruel aspect, often as Medusa in the poems. In sonnet 310, Petrarch depicts a Spring scene which alludes to the Springtime festival of Floriana: in Ovid's *Fasti* (5.193-214), the god Zephyr chases Chloris: when he embraces her, flowers spill from her mouth. This sensual moment is depicted by Sandro Botticelli in his mysterious *Primavera* painting (Uffizi Gallery, Florence). But Petrarch's use of this sacred festival is to counterpoint the lushness with his own cold solitude and despondency.

Venus appears in many of Francesco Petrarch's poems: she is the Ancient Roman version of the Greek Aphrodite, Goddess of Love, mother of Cupid (who also appears in much of Petrarch's poetry and courtly love poetry). Her sacred flower is the red rose (these rain upon Laura in poem 126 of the *Rime Sparse*). There are two Venuses (from Plato in the *Symposium*): Sacred and Profane Love. In the Renaissance era, there was Venus Vulgaris and Venus Coelestis: one transcended from the Earthly to the Heavenly Venus.

Venus thus in Francesco Petrarch's mythopœia represents love in the act of transcendence. The movement in the art of Petrarch is usually from the earthly to the divine, and when he uses descriptions of Venus (such as from Virgil's *Aeneid*, in sonnet 90), he does so to suggest divine, angelic qualities which draw him up from Earth to Heaven.

Francesco Petrarch turns his eyes heavenward often: when he mentions the astrological aspects of planets such as Venus and Jupiter, he uses both the Neoplatonist's love of occultism, hermeticism and the significance of planets and numbers, and the Renaissance poet's love of Classical mythology (such as in poems 33 and 325).

Everything connects to everything else in the occult 'theory of correspondences': thus, gods are linked with planets, numbers, colours, jewels, days of the week, seasons and so on. Allusions to Venus or Cupid (Amor in Latin, Eros in Greek), link up with the dramas of Mars, Adonis, Jupiter, Diana, Psyche, Juno, Prosperine, Ceres and Mercury.

Francesco Petrarch's well-read poetic persona makes all these connections. The more allusions he can create with one word the better. Invoking Venus, or her opposite, the Virgin Goddess Diana, opens up a whole realm of mythology. As with William Shagspar's plays, there is a huge, teeming world of hermeticism and mythology behind Petrarch's poems. The lyrics read fine without the allusions, but they are so much richer with them.

TORN TO SHREDS

Love poets mythicize their experiences of love: thus poets continually anthropomorphize love, which becomes Cupid, Amor and Eros. Francesco Petrarch created the Triumph of Love, in his *Trionfi*: Love is a crowned, allegorical figure in a chariot in a procession. The poet puts love on a pedestal, turns it into allegory, myth, fable, story, moral, romance. Love becomes a Goddess, a cherub, an angel, a flower, a force of nature. In poem 78 of the *Canzoniere*, which commemorates the commission of Laura's portrait, the Petrarch-poet compares painting with sculpture (explicitly in sonnet 77): he alludes to the myth of King Pygmalion, who fell in love with a statue of Venus that he had made. The King prayed to the Goddess Venus for a woman as beautiful as the statue he'd created: Venus caused the statue to come to life.

How perfectly this myth describes the way artists fall in love with their creations, sometimes to the point of wanting to make love to them. The artist takes her/ his art in their embrace. The Pygmalion myth is deeply erotic, and speaks not only of the masculine desire to possess, but also of masturbation, fetishism, and narcissism (and also the blurring the boundaries in creating art, so that art and life become one).

The most erotic myth that Francesco Petrarch employs is that of Diana and Actæon. Like Orpheus and Dionysus the wine god, Actæon is torn to pieces. His crime is to disturb the Goddess Diana when she bathes in the woods. Ovid sets the scene in his lucid fashion:

> hic dea siluarum uenatu fessa solebat
> uirgineos artus liquido perfundere rore.
> (Here, the goddess of the woods, when exhausted from the hunt, to bathe her virgin limbs in the clear and dew-fresh water.[5]

The myth speaks of the pleasure of looking, of the eroticism of the (male) gaze, of breaking taboos, of moving into the sacred space of the Goddess (her holy grove in the trees, an inner sanctum of her landscape, which is her body). It is a myth of erotic transgression, where the male over-steps the delicate boundaries that lovers throw around around each other. Actæon's act is likened to rape – a breaking into the tabooed zone of the Goddess: he, instead, is raped.

There is further eroticism in the manner of Actæon's death: the hunter becomes the hunted, and feels what it is like to be preyed upon, as women so often are. Significantly, Actæon is turned into a stag, a very phallic animal. The death by his own hounds symbolizes the male being murdered by his own brute desires.

There is, too, a voluptuous masochism in Actæon's death, as there is in all sex-deaths. How beautiful to be a martyr, to die, ripped to shreds, like Dionysus being destroyed by his mænads. This is the masculine view, and it is very widespread: the apotheosis of such masochism is Christ's holier-than-holy suffering on the Cross.

Francesco Petrarch is attracted to such images of self-torture, partly because it elevates himself as a martyr. He makes significant changes to the myths, however. In poem 23 of the

Canzoniere, he uses six metamorphoses from Ovid. It is OK to be turned to stone, like Battus, or to be turned into a laurel, like Daphne, but Petrarch cuts out the death of himself as Actæon. Instead, he continues 'his project of praise'.[6]

Violence is not Francesco Petrarch's way, even though much of his poetry describes emotional violence. Love-deaths such as that of Actæon's were clearly too much for the Petrarchan poet.

Diana as Virgin Huntress is the opposite of Venus Goddess of love: Diana's arrows kill desire: Diana is chastity, opposing lust. She punishes Cupid. Being hunted by Diana must have flattered Petrarch's sensibilities, for love in his art has always been a battle between desire and repression, between lust for love and denial of it. He associated Diana, the chaste virgin, with the Madonna. Later, ironically, Diana became the Goddess of the witches among witchcraft cults of the Middle Ages.

Sometimes Francesco Petrarch turned around the hunter and the hunted, as in poem 190, where the poet hunts the white doe, sacred to Diana. In poem 323, which re-runs the themes of 23 in a different manner, Laura is hunted by the hounds of time, which kill her, as they kill everybody. The theme here is Laura's death in 1348, tho' the allusions are not buried, but made clear.

In *sestina* 237, Francesco Petrarch imagines himself to be Endymion, who was sent to eternal sleep by Jupiter. The youth was visited at night by the Moon Goddess and embraced. Diana takes over the role of Luna, and here assumes an undisguised erotic shape, in the sixth stanza:

> Ah, would that with the lover of the moon
> I had fallen asleep in some greenwood,
> and that she who before vespers gives me evening
> with the moon and with Love to that shore
> might come alone to stay there one night,
> and that the day and the sun might stay forever under the waves!

THE FINAL TRANSFORMATION

The Ovidian metamorphoses which Francesco Petrarch yearns to complete is that of being turned into a laurel, as in poem 23 in the *Rime Sparse*. The laurel, for Petrarch, as I've noted, joins together his notions of love, poetry, religion, mythology, vanity and morality. The laurel symbolizes victory, triumph, mortality, peace, and chastity, while in Christianity it is the crown of martyrdom. Laurels grow on top of Mount Parnassus, home of the Muses. The virtuous, evergreen laurel has one more meaning which is interesting but perhaps does not apply to Petrarch's complex web of Laura/ laurel meanings – the 'laurel was anciently believed to be prophylactic.'[7]

On one level, the laurel embodies Francesco Petrarch's aim for a total transformation of love, by love, in love, and through love. This is the ideal of courtly love, which aims at a whole body metamorphosis – body, soul, spirit, the complete person. As Conon de Bethune (d. 1219) said, love 'illumines and enflames my entire body';[8] and Arnaut Daniel spoke of being flooded with love.[9]

This serious theme of transcendence is not always treated solemnly. Early on in the sequence, in sonnet 5, Francesco Petrarch plays on the word *Laureta*, the latinized Laura. The semantic wordplay on Laura/ *l'aura* and so on helps to exalt Petrarch's poetic sense of self, as Sandra Berman noted in *The Sonnet Over Time* (29-30).

The metamorphoses that Francesco Petrarch aims to undergo have affinities with the processes of alchemy. Poetry is alchemy; both poetry and alchemy are forms of magical transformations. In alchemy, the initiate searches for the Philosopher's Stone, the union of the King and Queen, the creation of gold and cosmic unity. Alchemy aims at unification, taking base matter through the white, black and red transmutations.

In Francesco Petrarch's poetry and in much of love poetry the imagery is alchemical: the emphasis on fire, on burning and melting, on furnaces, heat, red, hearts and blood. The body thus becomes an alchemical vessel in which pain is transmuted into love. Narcissus turning into a flower is a kind of apotheosis – the flower of Narcissus, as Petrarch says in sonnet 45, is so lovely the grass is not worthy of it (45: 12-14).

The colours that Francesco Petrarch employs time after time – black, white, red and gold – are the colours of alchemy (in *canzone* 127, sonnets 46, 48, 90, 157, 165, 190, 265 and 291). In poems such as sonnet 175, Petrarch revived the troubadours' fiery imagery: the poet is 'all sulphur and tinder' and he is set alight by the beloved's words: the metaphors are alchemical, and hint at hidden processes that will transform the inner material of emotion, the heart, into pure gold. Thus, the living organ becomes eternal.

'A RAIN OF FLOWERS'

The most extraordinary scene, and certainly the most erotic, in the *Rime Sparse* is where a rain of flowers falls upon Laura. The scene is beatific, a glorification of the beloved; the eroticism is unveiled – the flowers fall upon her breasts, lap and skirt; the scene is Francesco Petrarch's clearest fusion of sex and mysticism:

> Da' be' rani scendea
> (dolce ne la memoria)
> unaspioggia di fior sovra 'l suo grembo,
>   et ella si sedea,
> umile in tanta gloria,
> coverta gia de l'amoroso nembo;
>   qual fior cadea sui lembo,
> qual su le treccie bionde
> ch'oro forbito et perle
> eran quel di a vederle,

qual si posava in terra et qual su l'onde,
qual con un vago errore
girando parea dir: "Qui regna Amore."
(From the lovely branches was descending (sweet in memory) a rain of flowers over her bosom, and she was sitting humble in such a glory, already covered with the loving cloud; this flower was falling on her skirt, this one on her blonde braids, which were burnished gold and pearls to see that day; this one was coming to rest on the ground, this one on the water, this one, with a lovely wandering, turning about seemed to say: "Here reigns Love". (40-52)

Francesco Petrarch's flowers crown Laura as a Queen of Heaven, a Goddess of Flowers, a glorified saint complete with nimbus or aureole. The roses fall from Heaven, as Petrarch says in sonnet 192: 'how much sweetness rains down on her' (3-4). In a pagan mode, Petrarch at the end of his major mythological poem in the *Canzoniere* (number 23), alludes to the shower of gold (Jupiter) that rained upon Danaë in Classical mythology (and related in Ovid's *Metamorphoses*, 4: 611). Renaissance depictions, such as by Mabuse, make this divine event erotic. In his poem, Francesco Petrarch denies being the rain of gold itself, but he is the 'flame lit by a lovely glance', the deity Semele whom Jupiter killed with his lightning during sex.

NINE

❧

THE ART OF POETRY

[Poets] sing truth… A certain divine power of spirit lodges in poets;
they cover the beauty of things with a teasing veil, which only a
(sharp eye can pierce…) [poets'] madness is divine. Dreaming is the
singer's right. Only when it soars can the soul, escaping mortality,
sing of exalted things…

Francesco Petrarch, *Epistolæ metricæ*[1]

Poetry is word magic; it is transformative magic; the original poet
was the dancing sorcerer, the prehistoric shaman.[2] Poetry can be a
religion, a mysticism, a way of life. 'All poetry is prayer',[3] said
Samuel Beckett, and this is true not only of religious poetry, but of
love poetry. The first poetry was religious, and poetry grew out of
religion and magic. In courtly love poetry, poetry becomes fused
again with religion.

All poetry, though, is mythic, magical, religious. The act of
writing/ making poetry is a magical act. For Rainer Maria Rilke,
poems were not just emotions, they were experiences.[4] The
magical view of poetry is espoused by or found in poets such as
Arthur Rimbaud, Paul Valéry, Robert Graves, Johann Wolfgang
von Goethe, Walt Whitman, Sappho, Gertrude Stein, Dante

Alighieri, the troubadours and Francesco Petrarch.

Mircea Eliade sums up best the magical nature of poetry in his excellent book *Shamanism*:

> Poetic creation still remains an act of perfect spiritual freedom …The purest poetic act seems to re-create language from an inner experience that, like the ecstasy or the religious inspiration of 'primitives', reveals the essence of things. (510)

Francesco Petrarch, like Dante Alighieri and the troubadours, believes in the magical powers of poetry, while at the same time remaining doubtful of the power of anything, including God. Petrarch is restless, and though he hopes for magical transformations, he knows they may never happen. To make them occur, he knows, as all poets do, that he has to try harder, to make better and better poetry, to extend his language, his formal talent, so that the magical act of poetry becomes ever purer, more compressed, more revelatory, more illuminated, richer, deeper, and also clearer.

Paul Valéry, speaking of Stéphane Mallarmé, wrote:

> Language thus becomes an instrument of "spirituality" …of the direct transmutation of desires and emotions into presences and powers that become 'realities' in themselves.[5]

Francesco Petrarch too believes in the spiritualization of language. Petrarch is one of those poets, like Paul Valéry, Stéphane Mallarmé, Rainer Maria Rilke, Giraut de Borneil, Gertrude Stein and Robert Graves, who is a 'poet's poet', who holds that poetry has a mystical dimension that manifests itself when poetry is progressively refined. Like Valéry and Rilke, among modern poets, and Cavalcanti, Guinicelli and Dante of his own era, Petrarch continually refines poetry, making it clearer and clearer, purer and purer. Even when he is being obscure, as in the troubadour *trobar clus* or 'closed style', he is being clear, as he explains in a letter of 1352:

You command me to write in a clear style; and I have every wish to obey you in everything. But on one point we disagree. What you call "clear" is something close to the ground; I think that the higher the style the clearer, provided it doesn't get involved in its own clouds.[6]

PURE POETRY

French writers such as Gustave Flaubert, Stendhal, Stéphane Mallarmé, Arthur Rimbaud, André Gide and Paul Valéry dreamt of a language that would be reduced to pure essence, that would communicate clearly, free of artifice, trickery, obscurity and ornament.

Francesco Petrarch is, similarly, an advocate of pure poetry. Umberto Bosco says that Petrarch's poetry is 'non-immediate', meaning it is always composed after the event (*Petrarcha*, 166). True, and this is partly because, as well as being a poet of memory, like C.P. Cavafy, Petrarch also desires to control every aspect of artistic creation. He wants nothing hurried or gushing. He does not gush like Henry Miller or Arthur Rimbaud. His poetry is always controlled. He shapes his emotion meticulously, spending a good deal of time editing and re-editing the poems.

This rigorous self-control is seen also in his letters, which are not explosive, immediate outbursts, but orchestrated pieces of literature. Francesco Petrarch is a poet of ecstatic self-analysis, like C.P. Cavafy, William Shakespeare and Heinrich Heine. Like André Gide, Petrarch knows that everything he feels can become art. Petrarch scrutinizes himself, his desires, ideas and emotions. As Edgar Quintet wrote, in 1878:

> Petrarch's originality consists in having realized, for the first time, that every moment of our existence contains in itself the substance of a poem, that every hour encloses an immortality.[7]

In Francesco Petrarch's work, every gesture can become art: Petrarch's aim is to develop a pure art that captures every nuance of his body and soul's experiences. Adolfo Bartoli spoke (in *Petrarcha,* 1884) of Petrarch's 'self-scrutiny ...turning every impulse into art.'[8]

The aim of a pure poetry is exceptionally difficult to achieve, and so few poets have even come close. Francesco Petrarch was a rigorous reviser of poems, as E.H. Wilkins notes in his life of Petrarch: he 'made a hundred or so changes in *canzone* 268' (77-78). This can be normal practice for a poet, for any artist.

For many critics, Francesco Petrarch's self-consciousness is his major contribution to poetry.[9] Petrarch's great realization was that poetry is crucially important in itself, and does not need to refer to anything else to attain completeness. Poetry, he understood, could be self-sufficient. This does not mean that Petrarch thought art could exist in a vacuum: he knew that art works better if it is grounded in experience, in realities and in intense feelings.

For him, these feelings were in the realm of love. Francesco Petrarch knew that he was partly inventing the feelings of love he felt. As C.P. Cavafy said, 'Art is what the artist invents.'[10] The emphasis in Petrarch's *œuvre*, as with Samuel Beckett, James Joyce and many other modernists, is on invention, on the richness of the artistic imagination.

THE POETICS OF PETRARCH

Francesco Petrarch's poetics pivot around the relation between art and life, between artifice and real experience, between the ideal art object and the actual beloved woman, Laura. One of the extraordinary aspects of Petrarch's poetry is its introspection, sustained over hundreds of sonnets, 29 *canzoni*, 7 *ballate*, 9 *sestine* and 4 *madrigali*. Other poets (all poets) had been introspective before Petrarch, but not in quite the same self-indulgent, highly refined, sweet manner.

What strikes the reader of the *Rime Sparse* is that Laura is a pretext for poetry (just like Beatrice in Dante Alighieri's *Vita Nuova*), just as much (if not more) than being the object and goal of the poetry. As Adolfo Bartoli put it in *Petrarca*, Francesco Petrarch 'objectivates his subjective states... [Laura] is merely the reflection of his spirit.' (253) It turns out, as Thomas Bergin writes in *Petrarch*, Laura is not required at all for some of the poems, except 'as a memory to sharpen his melancholy perception.' (167)

The introspective nature of the *Canzoniere* has models – Dante Alighieri's *Vita Nuova*, for instance, where Dante explains each poem and how it relates to his interiorization. Francesco Petrarch's develops the poetics of introspection further, and refines it to the point of self-parody and decadence. At so many points Petrarch's glittering edifice threatens to collapse. In poems such as sonnet 5, Petrarch dazzles with his rich wordplay. There are times, though, when the poems in the *Rime Sparse* are too sweet, too refined, too self-conscious, too sophisticated and too intelligent.

Is it possible to be too intelligent? Yes, when the cleverness takes over and there is little else in a poem except artifice and scholasticism.

Some poems are so sweet and breathless they become laughable. Love makes fools of people, as all love poets realize. And Francesco Petrarch, ironic though he is most of the time, can nevertheless make a fool of himself. The second part of the *Canzoniere* in particular is full of emotional cries which seem to fall on the wrong side of irony, such as in sonnet 298, where the poet laments thus:

> O mia Stelle, o Fortuna, o Fato, o Morte,
> o per me sempre dolce Giorno et crudo,
> come m'avete in basso stato messo!
> (O my Star, O Fortune, O Fate, O Death, O Day
> to me always sweet and cruel,
> how you have put me in low estate.)

The sweetness is part of the torture, for the more the poet recalls the sweetness of his beloved, the bitterer is his sorrow. Love poetry is full of such sad cries, for love is painful and lovers, like babies, cry when they are hurt.

At the same time, Francesco Petrarch lacks a mature sensibility in his inability to transcend the vagaries of love. Earlier poets, such as Sappho, Catullus and the Greek epigrammatists wrote in bitter, ironic terms about love. The Petrarch-poet might benefit from more mature distancing and less rhetorical flourishes.

The form of Francesco Petrarch's poetry is much admired, however – the antitheses, musicality, alliteration (using consonants), metaphors, and rich wordplay (as in this line (5) from sonnet 303: 'fior, frondi, erbe, ombre, antri, onde, aure soavi' = 'flowers, leaves, grass, shadows, caves, waves, gentle breezes').[11] Petrarch's formal and technical skills are unsurpassed. In the *canzoni* and *sestine* he is especially dazzling. Yet he did not invent any new poetic forms (S. Minta, 2-3). In some ways, he was formally conservative (conservatism is reflected in his political beliefs, in his view of love). Yet in the sonnet form he excelled as few poets have done since (Shakespeare, Baudelaire and Rilke have written amazing sonnets, for instance).

TEN

ક્ર

CONCLUSION:
PETRARCH AND LOVE POETRY

Veramente siam nol polvere et ombra;
Veramente la voglia cieca e 'ngorda;
Veramente fallace e la speranza.
(Truly, we are dust and shadow; truly, desire is blind and greedy;
truly, hope deceives.)

Francesco Petrarch, *Rime Sparse,* sonnet 294 (12-14)

THE COURTLY LOVE IDEAL

The ideals of courtly love can be assessed in part from the visual
images of the era: the knight chivalrously leaving on the
Crusades; knights jousting and tilting; the wooden (and later,
stone) castles; the dances in the gardens of love; wife-beating (in a
number of pictures, as from the *Roman de la Rose*[12]); hunting;
falconry; musicians, minstrels and *jongleurs* singing and playing
pipes, drums, lutes, flutes, fiddles and viols; the patterned
backgrounds to illuminations – the rooms decorated in blue or
red, with small squares, *fleur-de-lis* and criss-crosses; the candid

images of 'the lover and his lady' – the woman inelegantly climbing into bed (such as in the *Roman d'Artus*[13]); people in the mediæval manuscripts are also shown eating, praying, riding on horseback, reading and sometimes women are seen leading dragons.

In the images of the Middle Ages, people go about their lives solemnly. They are seldom depicted smiling or laughing. Life seems to be a serious matter. The people are blissfully self-absorbed, unconscious of being painted (so different from the smug knowingness of post-Renaissance models). Middle Ages images have a quiet charm about them, an ornamental beauty, poise, delicacy and simplicity; this is true of the lavish *Book of Hours of the Virgin* of some feudal lord, and also a picture of a everyday, interior scene.

Francesco Petrarch is essentially a courtly love poet. The spaces of his poems – the pastoral landscapes of the Vaucluse, the fountains and rivers, the woods and walks – are those of the troubadours' poems. Petrarch's codes of love are those of *fin amor*. It was Giraut de Borneil who most lucidly summarized the function of the courtly love poet, in one of his highly compressed but vivid *cansos*:

> Amars, onrars, e char-teners,
> Umiliars et obezirs,
> Loncs merceiars e loncs grazirs,
> Long'attans'e loncs espers
> Me degron far viur'ad onor,
> S'eu fos astrucs de bo senhor,
> Mas car no'm vir ni no'm biais,
> No vol Amors qu'eu sia gais.
> (Loving, honouring and holding dear, acting humbly and obeying, long asking for grace and long making gracious approaches, long paying of attentions and long hoping should cause me to live in honour, if I were blessed with a good master. But because I do not turn back or bend. Love does not wish that I should be in joy.)[14]

Love rules as a God over people in courtly love. In the work of Andreas Capellanus *(The Art of Courtly Love)*, usually taken as one of the key writers of courtly love (though Peter Dronke disagrees),[15] women have an equal role to play, as 'servants of the god of love'.[16] As with Francesco Petrarch and Dante Alighieri, the key element in courtly love is, as A.J. Denomy wrote, 'an ever unsatisfied, ever increasing desire'.[17] In the the poetry of the troubadours, this desire is clearly as much erotic as spiritual. The Countess of Dis wrote:

> My heart and love I offer him,
> my mind, my eyes, icy life.
> ...If only I could lie beside you for an hour.[18]

Courtly love is all unsatisfied desire, distance, projection, lack, self-loathing, servitude, despair and death. Courtly love operates around the eroticism of the poet, the poet's look, the psychic pressure that the poet brings to bear upon the beloved by the force and eloquence of her/ his poetry. The upswelling of love poetry is found across much of Europe in the Middle Ages. The German *Minnesängers* were just as yearning and desirous as the troubadours, as Heinrich von Mobrungen attests in one of his lyrics:

> She has wounded me;
> in my innermost soul,
> within the mortal core,
> when I told her
> that I was raving and anguished
> in desire for her glorious lips.[19]

The voluptuous martyrdom of the troubadours, where they are wounded in their hearts by arrows which spill the blood of love, was refined in the *stil novisti* poets, and in Dante Alighieri and Francesco Petrarch. Sex was gradually spiritualized, intellectualized, sublimated. But eroticism still welled up in the poetry of Dante and Petrarch, as we have seen: in the dream of the bloody heart in the *Vita Nuova*, and in the fantasy image of the red roses falling on Laura in the *Rime Sparse*, to cite two of the more vivid examples.

In their effort to expunge eroticism from poetry, Dante Alighieri and Francesco Petrarch realized that desire has a sexual component that cannot be wholly denied. Indeed, it helps to give desire and love poetry an authentic edge which it might not otherwise possess.

WOMEN IN COURTLY LOVE POETRY

At first sight, it seems as if women fare better in courtly love culture and courtly love poetry than in earlier philosophies and codes of love. In courtly love, women are ecstatically eulogized. Bernart de Ventadour is typical among the troubadours in his apostrophizing of the beloved, thus:

> I love my lady so much and hold her dear, I fear her so much, and respect her, that I never dared speak to her of myself, nor seek anything nor ask anything of her.[20]

The troubadours are such sweet martyrs, silently suffering so honourably in their love for women. Troubadour poetry is interpreted in a number of ways. Bernart de Ventadour's "De l'aiga que dels olhs plor", for instance, is seen as Platonic love, religious allegory and an evocation of adultery by some critics.[21]

But whatever the socio-politico-historico-religious basis for troubadour poetry, the exaltation of women is paramount. This poetry of praise continues through the *dolce stil novo* of the 14th century to the Elizabethan sonneteers of the late 1500s and beyond to the Romantics of the early 1800s.

It all seems to be so good for women, all this praise from men. In the poesie of Guido Cavalcanti, Dante Alighieri and Francesco Petrarch, women are praised even higher – they become, no less, angels and divine beings. In the *dolce stil novo,* women are raised and praised higher than in most poetry. In Guido Cavalcanti's "In un baschetto", a *ballata* in a 'pastourelle' mode, the sublimation of sexuality is seen clearly, as is the fusion of love, women, nature and divinity:

> She took me by the hand, to show her love,
> and told me she had given me her heart.
> She guided me to a fresh little grove,
> where I saw flowers of every colour bloom;
> and I felt so much joy and sweetness there,
> I seemed to see the god of love descending.[22]

Courtly love is regarded by (mainly male) critics as nothing short of a revolution, compared to which, as C.S. Lewis wrote in *The Allegory of Love*, 'the Renaissance is a mere ripple on the surface of literature.' (12) For some critics, *fin amor* was 'an essential stage in the emancipation of women' (Claude Marks in *Pilgrims, Heretics and Lovers*).[23]

Female critics see the whole thing differently: 'Throughout the Middle Ages women were the pawns of men', asserted Meg Bogin in *The Women Troubadours* (10). Rape was common not just for peasant women but also for the aristocracy, stuck in their claustrophic castles.[24] Rape must surely have been as common then as it is now: domestic violence counts for about 25% of all violence.[25] Squashed in together in the castles and houses, men would have had plenty of opportunities for sexual assault. Poets counter-acted such urges by raising women to the highest realms. The pain of women became the pain of men. The emotional shift of the 'blame' from women to men occurs throughout courtly love poetry, and in that of the early Italian poets.

Thus Bonaggiunta Urbiciani writes:

> Love rends apart
> My spirit and my heart,
> Lady, in loving thee[26]

and Jacopo de Lentino says:

thou, lady, killest me,
Yet keepest me in pain. (In ib., 43)

This shift of pain is found throughout the work of Dante and Petrarch, too. Even when she is at her most angelic, in the *Paradiso*, Beatrice is still the woman of courtly love who kills with her eyes, the *femme fatale* of Western literature:

Then Beatrice looked at me, her eyes
  sparkling with love and burning so divine,
  my strength of sight surrendered to her power –

With eyes cast down, I was about to faint.
(*Paradiso*, IV: 139-142)

The spiritualization of women in the poems of the Italian poets – in the work of Dante Alighieri, Francesco Petrarch, Guinicelli, Cavalcanti, Cino da Pistoia – is even more detrimental in some ways than the glorification of women in the work of troubadour poets. The troubadours at least exalted real people, with faults and powers. The women of the troubadours were at least often in positions of social power; some ran courts alone.[27] In the *dolce stil novo* poets, women are severely abstracted: their bodies, hopes, desires and problems were denied. The women of courtly love poetry were flesh and blood; the women of the *dolce stil novo* were reduced to a pair of vicious, dazzling eyes. The ethereal, deified women of the Italian mediæval poets are abstracted from reality so much that they became props of poetry. They are ungrounded in the realities that make love a rich and valuable experience. Women in the art of Dante and Petrarch are pure desires, as Meg Bogin explained in *The Women Troubadours*:

Desexed and beatified (Beatrice), definitively changed into man's spiritual redeemer, the lady of the poets became the mannequin with which all women were compared. Perhaps the elevation of the lady was a major turning point in the history of man; to consider this development a positive one for women would be to ignore its crippling effect on the women of succeeding centuries, including our own. (16)

Like the supermodels of today's magazines (*Vogue, Elle, Marie Claire, Bliss*), the women of courtly love poetry and the *dolce stil novo* were idealized, fantasized women which real women can never emulate. They are impossible ideal figures that extract all the rawness, the wildness, the creativity, the complexity and strength of real people.

The Goddesses of the ancient world – Isis, Aphrodite, Diana, Ishtar, Kali, Astarte, Anu – were vivacious, powerful figures. Even though they were largely the creations of patriarchal culture (not all of which is instituted by men), at least they had moments of real wildness and magical transformation. The Western Goddess of the mediæval age, the Virgin Mary, is a pale, passive, watered-down incarnation of the ancient Goddesses. Only at times, and these are rare, does the Madonna take on some of the savage aspects of the ancient Goddesses – when she is the woman of the Apocalypse, for instance (*Revelations*, 12: 1).

The Virgin Mary is a solemn, passive Goddess, solely a nurturer and mother, and the architecture of the cities where her cult flourished is also solemn, dark, heavy (Chartres, Paris, Bruges, Cologne). Francesco Petrarch is a Southern European – and his landscapes are more like those of Greek mythology: the shrines of Diana at Ephesus, for instance.

Francesco Petrarch's vision of the Blessed Virgin comes from the city culture of Dante Alighieri, rather than the Provençal heretical cults such as the Cathars, which were founded in the soil of Southern France. Petrarch's poetic world is distinctly city-based (although the settings might be the villages of the Vaucluse).[28]

THE TRANSCENDENCE OF LOVE IN FRANCESCO PETRARCH'S POETRY

The final act of transcendence in the *Canzoniere* is to go beyond human love to divine love, embodied in the figure of the Virgin Mary. Like so many poets of the era, Francesco Petrarch finds salvation in the motherly presence of Our Lady. For him, the Madonna is a sanctuary, a shelter from life's cruelties. She is the Madonna della Misericordia, as painted so memorably by Piero della Francesca (1445, Sansepulcro). Piero's deity is a severe, aloof Mother of Mercy, who seems to regard herself as far superior to the humans she shelters.

Francesco Petrarch's Madonna is similarly proud and stern. All through the *Rime Sparse*, Petrarch has been caught between lust and despair, between seeing human love as sin and love as divine: in the final poems, he switches to God, to renouncing his worldly self, his love of Laura de Sade, his desire for an earthly apotheosis. The final poem is an extraordinary hymn to the Virgin Mary, one of the most powerful there is. He exalts her as *Vergine bella, Vergine saggi, Vergine pura, Vergine santa, Vergine sola al mondo, Vergine chiara* and *Vergine umana*. She is, for him, a Goddess, a Star of the Sea, bright, merciful, a guide, chaste, sweet, wise, the Queen of Heaven.

Francesco Petrarch uses the same language, the same means of praise for the Madonna as for Laura de S. Petrarch separates Laura from the Virgin Mary, and aims his pleas at the Madonna. This change is only half-convincing, even though Petrarch has been repenting all through the *Rime Sparse*. In the last of the *Triumphs*, he wrote:

> If he was blest who saw her here on earth,
> What will it be to see her again in Heaven.[29]

This is the traditional, Christian stance: that life will be made blissful only through death. It is the ethic of Dante Alighieri in the *Vita Nuova* and *The Divine Comedy*. Transcendence ultimately only occurs in death – in and through death. The agent and energy may be love (Love as God), but death is the gateway, the method, the road.

This is where poets such as Dante Alighieri and Francesco Petrarch differ from other love poets. For the non-Christian love poet (Sappho, William Shakespeare, C.P. Cavafy), love is enough in itself, and ecstasy of the love union is the end-point. With Christian poets, and with mystics such as the Sufis and those of Judaism, there has to be something more. Love is not enough, is not an end in itself, for religious poets: there is always God, a deity, something divine, and any transcendence must involve God or deities. Mysticism speaks always of a beyond, it is towards this that the religious poet strives. Thus Jalal al-Din Rumi writes:

> this is Love: to fly heavenward,
> to rend, every instant, a hundred veils.[30]

Francesco Petrarch and Dante Alighieri are not this violent in their God-centred mysticism and transcendence. Their entry into Heaven is envisaged as a decorous procession amid lilies and roses, with angels smiling brightly and the whole of Heaven bathed in stagey, white light.

The more fervent Catholic mystics, such as St Bernard, St Catherine and St Teresa, emphasized the power of love. St Bernard famously wrote: 'I love because I love; I love in order that I may love',[31] while one of the finest modern theologians, Bernard Lonergan, said that: 'the experience of being-in-love is an experience of fulfilment, of complete integration'.[32]

Dante Alighieri and Francesco Petrarch, however, like so many Christian mystics, do not stop at love. Like mystics who dreamt of a marriage with the Virgin Mary – a blasphemous but longed-for event – the Dante-poet and the Petrarch-poet yearn to transcend the limits of human love, and move up into a world of pure, rarefied, refined love, which is the love between Christ and Mary, the soul and God.

So Francesco Petrarch renounced earthly love. It seems to us now neurotic that he should so violently repent, so violently damn his former love. But for the spiritual sublimation to work effectively, it seems it must be violent. This is typical, anyway, of Christian theologians, who have always spoken of repentance and sin in aggressive terms. What must not happen, of course, is the sinner who repents of repenting, that is, going back on her/himself. The switch must be total. Speaking of his former love for Laura, Petrarch says, in a letter to Luca Cristian of 1349:

> Thus were composed those songs in Italian of my young distress, of which I now repent with shame, although they seem to be very welcome to those who suffer from the same disease.[33]

Seeing love as a disease is a familiar Christian, if psychotic, view. Francesco Petrarch was confused, to the end, it seems, by the whole question of love. He believed life was a matter of Heraclitean strife,[34] and, worse, that even in the midst of life we are dying – another familiar (and masculine) view: 'we are both dying, everyone is dying'.

In the *De remediis utriusque fortune*, Francesco Petrarch wrote that

> love is a hidden fire, a pleasing wound, a sweet bitterness, a delightful disease, an agreeable torture, a charming death.[36]

Familiar ideas on love, which are echoed throughout the Western world – in the outpourings of the Marquis de Sade, Paul Éluard and James Joyce.

Francesco Petrarch discussed his conflict most fully in the *Secretum* in which he pits his wits against St Augustine, who is of course the ideal questioner in this inquisition. Petrarch (Franciscus) begins:

> I have never loved her body so much as her soul. My delight was in her character, transcending mortality, resembling that of the angels.

This is not good enough for Augustine, who retorts:

> She's a queen, a saint, if you like, or as Virgil said, a goddess, a sister of Phoebus, a nymph. But her great virtue will not help to excuse your errors.

To which Franciscus replies: 'Whatever I am due is to her.' A few pages later, St Augustine weighs in again on the familiar topic of love and sex as sin and death:

> She has distracted your mind from the love of the Creator and has turned it to the love of the creature... Love has made you wretched; that's what I began by saying. Earthly love leads to forgetfulness of God; it has brought you to the miserable state you have described.[37]

This torment is self-created. Religionists fanatically defend their faith against others: any other form of love must be no good, simply because it is not going towards God, towards *their* God. Christians think God is greedy: he must have all the love that's around for himself (but if he's so complete and perfect, why does he need to be loved so much?).

There are, of course, many forms of love that are much more useful than love of God: motherly love, love of friends, and humanity. Each of these loves is more noble, more dignified, more spiritual, more important and more useful than love of God. Nevertheless, it is love of God that Dante Alighieri and Francesco Petrarch and so many poets put above all other kinds of love. Their theory is that every other form of love flows from God's love. This view only works if God stands at the centre of it. Take away God, as people did after the Renaissance, then the whole edifice crumbles.

Dante Alighieri believed that humans have a threefold spirit – the vegetable, the animal and the rational. Sexual pleasure is of the animal stage; clearly Dante and Francesco Petrarch favoured the rational sphere:

> insofar as he is rational, he [man] seeks what is right, in which he is

alone, or else ranked with the angels.[38]

Dante Alighieri, like Francesco Petrarch, would prefer to walk with the angels, but he realized that all three elements of the human condition have to be dealt with. Petrarch, in denying the lower stages of humanity, the baser aspects of life, aimed to refine himself into a state of spiritual transcendence. In the *Letter to Posterity*, he acknowledges that much of human life is pure vanity ('youth and pleasures are vain').[39] When he is in this Augustinian mode, nothing less than the purest, most exquisitely refined thought will do. In this mood, St Paul and St Augustine win out over Cicero and Virgil, and spirit triumphs over flesh.

Sometimes the vanity topples over into self-hatred, and the humility demanded by Christian ethics becomes all-important. In the *De Otio religioso*, Francesco Petrarch wrote:

Nothing is impossible to God; in me there is total impossibility of rising, buried as I am in such a great heap of sins. He is potent to save; I am unable to be saved.[40]

There is no way out of such paradoxical emotional states. And in Francesco Petrarch's philosophy the Augustinian conflict between love and sin, between God and sex, is further deepened, because Augustine in his *Confessions* links the sins of the flesh with the abuse of words and the reading of pagan letters.[41] What this means is that reading the Classics can be sinful, and encourages sinfulness. In Augustine's view, anything that deflects the soul from God is sinful. Much of early Christian teaching denies life, hates the richness of life.

Francesco Petrarch's torment stems from his personality, his culture, his religion, his poetics and his philosophy. For him, as for another tormented Catholic soul, André Gide, æsthetics and ethics are the same thing. Art is morality. In Petrarch's world-view, the concepts of love, sin, God, Laura, poetry and religion are bound up together so tightly it is impossible to extract one or another without altering the whole. Petrarch's poetics must therefore be morally, metaphysically and spiritually utterly right. No ambiguity must creep in. But the whole of metaphysics, morality, spirituality and poetics are highly ambiguous.

In Francesco Petrarch's poetics, the ice/ fire anti-theses reflect a larger and deeper ambivalence which lies at the heart of his art, and his life. Laura herself becomes a pretext for a spiritual exploration in which the essence of poetry is explored as much as the essence of religion and love. Laura, in fact, as Sandra Berman notes in *The Sonnet Over Time*

> passes into a distant, if erotically charged plane of words, all artistically molded, all ultimately referring more to the speaker's than to Laura's experience.[42]

Eventually, in the art of Francesco Petrarch, poetry assumes a massive significance, and poetic purity is valued as highly spiritual purity. In Hindu mysticism, the seer and the Seen are often one (in the *Bhagavad-Gita*);[43] that is, the soul and the Divine Ground are often the same thing, ultimately. In the philosophy of Petrarch, as in Dante's philosophy, the questing soul (the poet) and the beloved (the woman) are also one. Beatrice and Laura become simply parts of Dante and Petrarch. They are part of the poets anyway, already, as they only exist in any real sense in the texts themselves (and in all the criticism that comes after the poems).

In Western mysticism, at the height of the mystical union, the self and God are one – 'are one is', as Meister Eckhart put it.[44] In the mythopœia of Dante Alighieri and Francesco Petrarch, the poet and the beloved are 'one is', and the 'is' is the poem. What we have with Dante and Petrarch and the troubadours are not great artists. The poets themselves are long gone, long dead. What we have are great poems. The poems live on. And one suspects that this is *exactly* what Petrarch, and Dante, perhaps, would have wished more than anything.

APPENDIX

è.

ON PETRARCHISM

A word or two ought to be said about Petrarchism. Firstly, many critics argue that Francesco Petrarch's influence was massive and widespread. He influenced much of the English sonnet tradition, for example, as found in poets such as Sir Philip Sidney, Edmund Spenser, Samuel Daniel, Henry Constable and Michael Drayton. It was the wonderful poet Sir Thomas Wyatt who famously developed the Italian sonnet form, and was key in introducing it into English poetry.

Francesco Petrarch's influence can be seen in later British poets, such as John Donne, Henry Vaughan, Andrew Marvell, John Milton, John Keats, Percy Shelley and Robert Graves. It was William Shakespeare who most famously really got to grips with the Petrarchan sonnet and Petrarchan poetics. Shakespeare developed Petrarchan poetics far beyond anything that had gone on before (although Shakespeare was coming late to the fashion for sonneteering in English culture). In Shakespeare's poetry the sonnet sequence reaches its apotheosis, in the same way that Petrarch crowns, and ends, the courtly love ideal, as J.H. Whitfield noted in *A Short History of Italian Literature*.[1]

In *Romeo and Juliet,* William Shakespeare alludes affectionately to Petrarch and Laura (II, iv, 38f). In sonnet 30 of the *Sonnets*, Shagspur mocks the Petrarchan conceits ('My mistress' eyes are nothing like the sun', and so on). Shakespeare's *Sonnets* are so fleshly and erotic, Petrarch would probably be repulsed by them. Yet no one else, apart from Shakespeare, comes close to the magic and power of Petrarch's sonnet sequence.[2]

Francesco Petrarch's influence is largely a poetic one; that is, poets after Petrarch admired his control, his flourishes, his style, his ability to organize a group of poems into a coherent structure, his conceits, his wordplay and his moralistic concept of poetics. The love content in the works of Petrarch is nothing new. I've said that Sappho and Catullus covered much the same ground in the ancient world. Sappho, in particular, captures the erotic force and frenzy of love so well, and in such a highly compact manner, as in her famous fragment:

> Once again Love, the loosener of limbs,
> shakes me, that sweet-bitter creature.[3]

Or in this fragment, which demonstrates Sappho's astonishing way of picking exactly the right metaphor:

> Love shook my heart,
> like the wind falling on oaks on a mountain.

Among European poets, Francesco Petrarch's influence is certainly easy to see in poets such as Maurice Scève, Pierre Ronsard, Torquato Tasso, Joachim Du Bellay, Giovanni Battista Marino and Pietro Bembo. In his *dizains* (10-line poems), Scève (1500-1564) echoes Petrarch's poetry many times. He burns and burns while the beloved thrives (*dizain* 7); his love goes through storms and darknesses (24, 58); and at times Sceve's yearning bursts through the mannered, supple web of Petrarchan conceits and wordplay to produce poems such as *dizain* 161:

> Seul avec moy, elle avec sa partie:

moy en ma peine, elle en sa molle couche.
Convert d'ennuy je me voultre en l'Ortie,
et elle nue entre ses bras se couche.
(Here alone I lie, there she and he,
I on my bed of pain, on soft sheets she;
my weary flesh sprawled on rancorous nettles,
hers on its nakedness folded in his arms.)[4]

Like Francesco Petrarch, Maurice Scève compared his beloved to Goddesses (Diana, Hecate, Luna, etc); like Petrarch, he enjoys the torture of his love in a luxurious, masochistic fashion; this sense of exquisite self-mortification occurs in the poesie of Torquato Tasso. In one of his lyrics, Tasso wrote of a beloved not unlike Laura:

O via più bianca fredda
di lei che spesso fa parer men bele
col suo splendor le stelle;
turba il suo puro argento
o nube o pioggia o vento,
nulla il tuo liata giri
sia la mia vita un sogno edio contento.
(O whiter and colder far than her who often makes the stars less fair
with her shining; a cloud or rain or wind dims her pure silver,
nothing, your lovely whiteness and your fairest eyes. If you turn glad
to me, my life can be a dream and I be happy)[5]

What becomes clear in the poetry of Maurice Scève, Torquato Tasso, Giovanni Battista Marino, Joachim du Bellay, Pierre Ronsard and the Elizabethan sonneteers, is that Petrarchism is worn out even as it reaches the height of its popularity. And it becomes increasingly difficult to write an authentic love poem without slipping into artifice, parody and flatness. So the Romantic poets of the late 18th and early 19th centuries go even further, becoming more and more passionate and wild. After them, the tendency to go over-the-top to convince the reader of sincerity culminates in the Symbolists and Decadent lyricists in the 1880s and 1890s. In the 20th and 21st centuries there were/ are few poets who can write about love convincingly. Poets insist on falling in love, as most people do. But love becomes ever more difficult to describe or express in poetry, or in any literary art. Love is still a primary experience in poetry, but it is no longer possible to be convincing if you write, as Pierre Ronsard did in one of his *Sonnets For Hélène*:

> pour ce baiser tout plein,
> D'ambre, et de musq, baiser une Déasse
> (for that kiss full of
> amber and of musk,
> the kiss of a Goddess)[6]

In modern times, it is difficult to accept a poem composed in that lavish style. The Goddess is not a problem – she is being resurrected, reborn and renewed by a host of artists, pagans, witches, poets and New Age hippies. When Giovanni Battista Marino speaks of a laughing 'angelic little creature'[7] we have to forget the ornamental way of communicating and see through to the emotion beyond. What makes a poet like Sappho so fresh and immediate is that she wrote in such a clear, simple fashion. Sappho, and the Greek epigram writers, composed poetry in an uncluttered, direct way. There was little ornament, whereas Dante, Petrarch, the *stil novisti*, the troubadours and most of the Renaissance poets, are full of ornamentation and affectation.

Of course, a self-conscious obsession with form is not confined to the troubadours – one only has to think of the fragmentation of T.S. Eliot's *The Waste Land*, or Ezra Pound in his *Cantos*. The modernists, such as Pound, Gertrude Stein and Eliot, were inventing and re-inventing poetic forms in that quasi-serious, half-playful way which seems so modern, so in tune with the 21st century. In the works of Francesco Petrarch, Dante Alighieri and the troubadours, the forms and language seem now archaic and dated; but what they have to say of love is as up-to-date, as contemporary as it ever was. In pop songs of today, for instance, one finds the same Petrarchan conceits ('Baby, it's cold and raining outside, but you are warm in your bed', and so on), the same deification of women ('Baby, you're a Goddess!'), the same mix of sex and religion: in Eddie Gochran's 'Three Steps to Heaven', women and sex are the way to God, just as they were for the troubadours, and even Petrarch and Dante: Step One: you find a girl you love; Step Two: she falls in love with you; Step Three: you kiss and hold her tightly.

It's the same Petrarchan game of love, a process which sees the way to Heaven through the love and embrace of the beloved. The troubadours yearned for the affection of the beloved, because they knew that the love bed was also the God bed, that sex and religion fuse at many more points than the Catholic Church would care to acknowledge. Dante Alighieri, Petrarch and the *stil novisti* refined and spiritualized sexuality, but it was the same Three Steps to Heaven, the same transcendence through the beloved to the Great Beloved.

All contemporary pop songs do is to eroticize the language of love slightly, but it's the same yearning, the same desire for contact, the same longing for bliss. The only major difference between the pop singers of today and the courtly love poets of the Middle Ages is the method of consumption: love in pop music is blared out of giga-watt speakers in gigantic stadiums to crowds of thousands, or beamed across continents via satellites into millions of homes, or broadcast into cars during drive-time radio shows.

But much of pop music is consumed by people alone in their bedrooms and houses. Just like much of poetry. And in pop music, as in love poetry, one individual who is suffering because of love speaks directly and intimately to another person who knows something of the pain of love. Buddy Holly says it all in two lines from 'Maybe Baby':

Well, you are the one that makes me glad,
And you are one that makes me sad.

SIR THOMAS WYATT AND FRANCESCO PETRARCH

One can see Sir Thomas Wyatt's love poetry wholly in terms of Petrarchan poetics, if one wishes. Wyatt is, like Petrarch, very much a courtly love poet, a poet who professes, in his lyrics, the ethics of chivalry and courtesy. Like the troubadours, the *minnesängers* and the *stil novisti*, Wyatt aims for poetic refinement, codes of honour, nobility, loyalty and pride; like Bernart de Ventadour, Giraut de Borneil, Guido Guinicelli and Dante Alighieri, Wyatt writes at length of the beloved, espousing the traditional and so familiar notions of heterosexual, bourgeois romantic love. His yearning poet offers total devotion to the beloved woman, much as the saint kneels before the Virgin Mary. 'For yours I am,' he writes (in "My sweet, alas, forget me not"), 'Long have I loved her', he admits (in "Fortune, what aileth thee"), 'I am yours assuredly', he claims (in "The knot which first my heart did strain"), 'I was your thrall', he states in "Ye know my heart, my lady dear".

In Sir Thomas Wyatt's poesie, this thralldom is serious and relatively unquestioned; William Shakespeare, though, restlessly questions the notion of worshipping the beloved, emphasizing the sadomasochistic aspects of the lover-beloved relation. Shakespeare comments harshly and often bawdily on the master/ mistress-slave relation, while Wyatt pretty much accepts it as it is.

For Thomas Wyatt, the relation of mistress to lover is still noble, echoing the relation of knight or vassal to a lord, and saint to God. What powers Wyatt's love poetry, as with Francesco Petrarch's poesie, is loss of love, knowing the beloved once and now being estranged from her. Pain is the central experience in Wyatt's lyrics, the pain of not being with the beloved woman. She is elsewhere, so the poet consoles himself by writing poetry. Poetry is no consolation, though, and the more he writes the more dejected he becomes. As with Petrarch in his *Rime Sparse*, Wyatt in his love lyrics exacerbates and exaggerates the pain of love by making poetry out of it.

Sir Thomas Wyatt employs the Petrarchan conceit at length. His images are, typically, of fire and ice, of burning and freezing, of love and loss, straight out of the *Rime Sparse*. This passage from "At last withdraw your cruelty" is typical of Wyatt's Petrarchan imagery:

> For to the flame wherewith I burn
> My thought and my desire,
> When into ashes it should turn
> My heart by fervent fire
> You send a stormy rain
> That doth it quench again...

Each Wyatt love poem sets up oppositions, derived from Francesco Petrarch's example: the presence of the lover against the absence of the beloved; the cold Winter of agonizing loss outside the body against the hot Summer of burning desire inside the lover, and so on. Wyatt's protagonist lives in eternal sexual hardship:

> I toss, I turn, I sigh, I groan.
> My bed me seems as hard as stone
> ...For heat and cold I burn and shake...

...He writes in "What means this when I lie alone?", while in "The joy so short" he groans of 'endless pain'. At times, Wyatt sounds more like Francesco Petrarch than Petrarch himself.

The continuity between Francesco Petrarch and Sir Thomas Wyatt is emphasized by the fact that Wyatt translated Petrarch. Indeed, it was Wyatt, some claim, who introduced the courtly love/ *stil novisti* sonnet form into English poetry.

Michael Spiller writes in *The Development of the Sonnet*:

> the very first British writer to use the sonnet, Sir Thomas Wyatt, altered it very considerably: he made the first formal change in the structure of the sonnet since its invention in southern Italy in the early 13th century. (83-84)

Michael Spiller then goes to discuss Tom Wyatt's formal innovations, which included the alteration of the sestet from 3 + 3 to 4 + 2, ending with a rhymed couplet. It seems most probable that Wyatt, working with the *strambotti* of Srafino, was impressed by their epigrammatic neatness, and as a means of enforcing the wit and elegance of his own sonnets transferred the concluding couplet to his versions of the sonnets of Francesco Petrarch (ib., 85).

Sir Thomas Wyatt's versions of the *Rime Sparse* read like archetypal, English love poems. He made Francesco Petrarch's sonnets more ambiguous and abstract.[8] Wyatt's Petrarchan poems became the foundations of the Elizabethan sonnets. His version of Petrarch's sonnet 134 – "I find no peace" – reads thus:

> Pace non trobo e non ho da far guerra;
> E temo e spero, et ardo e sono un ghiaccio.
>
> I fynde no peace and all my warr is done;
> I fere and hope, I burne and friese like yse.

Compare the modes and images of Thomas Wyatt's love poems with Francesco Petrarch in, say, his sonnet (number 164) from his *Canzoniere*:

> veggio, penso, ardo, piango; et chi mi sface
> sempre m' e inanzi per mia dolce pena:
> guerra e 'l mio stato, d'ira e di duoi piena,
> et sol di lei pensando o qualche pace.
> (I am awake, I think, I burn, I weep; and she who destroys me is always before me, to my sweet pain: war is my state, full of sorrow and suffering, and only thinking of her do I have any peace.
> [*Petrarch's Lyric Poems*, 164: 5-8])

FRANCESCO PETRARCH

TIMELINE₁

1304.
Born at Arezzo, the 20th of July.

1305.
Is taken to Incisa at the age of seven months, where he remains seven years.

1312.
Is removed to Pisa, where he remains seven months.

1313.
Accompanies his parents to Avignon.

1315.
Goes to live at Carpentras.

1319.
Is sent to Montpellier.

1 Taken from Francesco Petrarch, *The Sonnets, Triumphs and Other Poems of Petrarch*, edited by Thomas Campbell, and published by George Bell & Sons, London, 1879.

1323.
Is removed to Bologna.

1326.
Returns to Avignon – loses his parents – contracts a friendship with James Colonna.

1327.
Falls in love with Laura.

1330.
Goes to Lombes with James Colonna – forms acquaintance with Socrates and Lælius – and returns to Avignon to live in the house of Cardinal Colonna.

1331.
Travels to Paris – travels through Flanders and Brabant, and visits a part of Germany.

1333.
His first journey to Rome – his long navigation as far as the coast of England – his return to Avignon.

1337.
Birth of his son John – he retires to Vaucluse.

1339.
Commences writing his epic poem, "Africa."

1340.
Receives an invitation from Rome to come and be crowned as Laureate – and another invitation, to the same effect, from Paris.

1341.
Goes to Naples, and thence to Rome, where he is crowned in

the Capitol – repairs to Parma – death of Tommaso da Messina and James Colonna.

1342.
Goes as orator of the Roman people to Clement VI. at Avignon – Studies the Greek language under Barlaamo.

1343.
Birth of his daughter Francesca – he writes his dialogues "De secreto conflictu curarum suarum" – is sent to Naples by Clement VI. and Cardinal Colonna – goes to Rome for a third and a fourth time – returns from Naples to Parma.

1344.
Continues to reside in Parma.

1345.
Leaves Parma, goes to Bologna, and thence to Verona – returns to Avignon.

1346.
Continues to live at Avignon – is elected canon of Parma.

1347.
Revolution at Rome – Petrarch's connection with the Tribune – takes his fifth journey to Italy – repairs to Parma.

1348.
Goes to Verona – death of Laura – he returns again to Parma – his autograph memorandum in the Milan copy of Virgil – visits Manfredi, Lord of Carpi, and James Carrara at Padua.

1349.
Goes from Parma to Mantua and Ferrara – returns to Padua, and receives, probably in this year, a canonicate in Padua.

1350.

Is raised to the Archdeaconry of Parma – writes to the Emperor Charles IV. – goes to Rome, and, in going and returning, stops at Florence.

1351.

Writes to Andrea Dandolo with a view to reconcile the Venetians and Florentines – the Florentines decree the restoration of his paternal property, and send John Boccaccio to recall him to his country – he returns, for the sixth time, to Avignon – is consulted by the four Cardinals, who had been deputed to reform the government of Rome.

1352.

Writes to Clement VI. the letter which excites against him the enmity of the medical tribe – begins writing his treatise "De Vita Solitaria."

1353.

Visits his brother in the Carthusian monastery of Monte Rivo – writes his treatise "De Otio Religiosorum" – returns to Italy – takes up his abode with the Visconti – is sent by the Archbishop Visconti to Venice, to negotiate a peace between the Venetians and Genoese.

1354.

Visits the Emperor at Mantua.

1355.

His embassy to the Emperor – publishes his "Invective against a Physician."

1360.

His embassy to John, King of France.

1361.

Leaves Milan and settles at Venice – gives his library to the Venetians.

1364.

Writes for Lucchino del Verme his treatise "De Officio et Virtutibus Imperatoris."

1366.

Writes to Urban V. imploring him to remove the Papal residence to Rome – finishes his treatise "De Remediis utriusque Fortunæ."

1368.

Quits Venice – four young Venetians, either in this year or the preceding, promulgate a critical judgment against Petrarch – repairs to Pavia to negotiate peace between the Pope's Legate and the Visconti.

1370.

Sets out to visit the Pontiff – is taken ill at Ferrara – retires to Arquà among the Euganean hills.

1371.

Writes his "Invectiva contra Gallum." and his "Epistle to Posterity."

1372.

Writes for Francesco da Carrara his essay "De Republica optime administranda."

1373.

Is sent to Venice by Francesco da Carrara.

1374.

Translates the Griseldis of Boccaccio – dies on the 18th of July in the same year.

NOTES

INTRODUCTION

1. See Stephen Minta: *Petrarch and Petrarchism*.
2. However, Petrarch had two children of his own: Giovanni (1337-61) and Francesca (b. 1343), by unnamed women.

CHAPTER ONE

1. P.T. Ricketts: *Les Poésies de Guilhelm de Montanhagol*, Toronto, 1964. no. 12; in A. Press, 273
2. 'The most important literary activity by women in the thirteenth century and much of the fourteenth was religious, flowering in the writing and dictation of mystical treatises.' (M.W. Labarge: *Women In Medieval Life*, 210.)
3. See Meg Bogin: *The Women Troubadours*.
4. See Weston La Barre: *The Ghost Dance*.
5. See Mircea Eliade: *A History of Religious Ideas*; and Joseph Campbell: *The Power of Myth*.
6. See Erich Neumann: *The Great Mother*, Bollingen/ Princeton University Press, New Jersey, 1972; Monica Sjöo & Barbara Mor: *The Great Cosmic Mother*, Harper & Row, San Francisco, 1987.
7. *Le Roman de la Dame à la Lycorne*, ed. Freidrich Gennrich, *Geselschaft fur romanische Litteratur*, 18, Dresden, 1908, 68-69.
8. Anonymous, 13th century, in Helen Waddell: *Medieval Latin Lyrics*, 253.
9. See Penelope Shuttle & Peter Redgrove: *The Wise Wound*, Paladin, 1986.
10. See Robert Graves: *Mammon and the Black Goddess*, Cassell, 1965:

'The Black Goddess represents a miraculous certitude in love' (162); see also Peter Redgrove: *The Black Goddess and the Sixth Sense*, Bloomsbury, 1987.

11. See John Harvey: *Medieval Gardens*, B.T. Batsford, 1981, plate VI.

CHAPTER TWO

1. C. Appel: *Bernart von Ventadorn*, XLIV, 9-12.

2. Jack Zipes: *Don't Bet On the Prince: Contemporary Feminist Fairy Tales in North America and England*, Gower, Aldershot, 1986, 258.

3. See Andrea Dworkin: *Pornography: Men Possessing Women*.

4. Larysa Mykyta, in *SubStance*, 39, 1983, 54.

5. Xavière Gauthier: "Pourquot Sorcières?", *in Sorcières*, no. l, 1976.

6. "A Question of Subjectivity: an interview" [with Susan Sellers], *Women's Review*, 12, 1986, in P. Rice, 1992, 133.

7. G. Cavalcanti: "Per gli occhi", in Maurice Valency, 1958, 239.

8. *Le Roman de la Rose*, tr. G. Dahlberg, Princeton University Press, New Jersey, 71.

9. See Lawrence Durrell, *A Smile in the Mind's Eye*, Wildwood House, 1980.

10. In *Selections From the Canzoniere*, tr. Mark Musa, 2.

11. In *The Life of Solitude*, tr. J. Zeitlin, Urbana, Illinois, 1924, 18.

12. G. Toja: *Arnaut Daniel's Canzoni*, Florence, 1960; and in L.T. Topsfield, *Troubadours and Love*, 214.

13. St Augustine: *De doctrina Christiana*, III, 10; and in J.P. Migne: *Patrilogiæ cursus completus*, 34, 72.

14. Thomas Aquinas: *Summa Theologica*, I-II, 26, art. 3.

15. St Bernard, *Sennpnes de diversis*, VIII, 9; and in J.P. Migne, 183, 565.

16. G. Boccaccio, *Decameron*, III, 10; see Stephen Booth: *Shakespeare's Sonnets*, Yale University Press, New Haven, 1977, 499.

17. Richard of St Victor, quoted in Peter Dronke: *Medieval Latin and the Rise of the European Love-Lyric*, I, 63-64.

18. Arnaut Daniel, op.cit., II, 25-6; in L. Topsfield, 208.

19. Pardigon, in F.J.M. Raynouard: *Choix des poesies originates des troubadours*, Paris, 1816-51, III, 344.

20. Sappho, in William Barnstone, tr., *Greek Lyric Poetry*, Schocken Books, New York, 1972, 93.

21. Quoted in Peter Dronke: *The Medieval Lyric*, 106.

22. A. Jeanroy, *Les Chansons de Guillaune IX*, C.

23. In Carl Appel: *Bernart de Ventadorn*, XXXV, 25; L.T. Topsfield, 118.

24. Hélène Cixous: "Le rire de le meduse", *Signs*, Summer, 1976.

25. In R.A. Nicholson: *Studies in Islamic Mysticism,* 324; and in Jack Lindsay, *The Troubadours and Their World*, 162.

26. Quoted in Peter Dronke: *The Medieval Lyric*, 89.

27. Plato, *Symposium,* tr. B. Jowett, in Maurice Valency, 27.

28. See Margaret B. Freeman, *The Unicorn Tapestries*, Metropolitan Museum of Art, New York. 1976, 42.

29. Dhu 'l-Nun, in A.J. Arberry, *Sufism*, 53.

30. In ib.,.60.

31. William Stoddart, *Sufism*, quoted in J. Robinson, *Blinded By tier Light*, 32.

32. R.W. Southern, *The Making of the Middle Ages*, Hutchinson, 1953, 219f.

33. Arnaut Daniel, quoted in Bernard O'Donoghue, 140-1.

34. See Linda M. Paterson, *Troubadours and Eloquence*, 140.

35. In Carl Appel, XLIII, 15-16; in L.T. Topsfield, 129.

36. A. Jeanroy: *Les Chansons de Guillaune IX*, I, 22-5; and in L.T. Topsfield, 46.

37. In G. Toja, X, 22-4; and in L.T. Topsfield, 206.

38. See Joseph Campbell, *The Power of Myth*.

39. In W.T. Pattison, *The Life and Works of the Troubadour Raimbaut d'Orange*, XVII, 38.

40. Olive Sayce, ed. *Poets of the Minnesang*, Oxford University Press, in B. O'Donoghue, 226-7.

41. Hans Denk, in Aldous Huxley, *The Perennial Philosophy,* Chatto & Windus, 1969, 282.

42. Quoted in Peter Dronke, *Medieval Latin*, 250.

CHAPTER THREE

1. In *Vita Nuova*, XIX, translated in *Dante's Lyric Poetry*, and in B. O'Donoghue, 286-7.

2. S.T. Coleridge, in David Wright: *English Romantic Verse*, Penguin, 1968, 184.

3. John Keats: 'Ode to Melancholy', *The Complete Poems*, ed. J. Barnard, Penguin, 1973.

4. "To Aphrodite", *Homeric Hymns,* 6, Putnam's Sons, New York, 1920, 427f.

5. In James B. Pritchard, ed. *Ancient Near Eastern Texts Relating to the Old Testament*, Princeton University Press, New Jersey, 1969, 383.

6. See Shirley Nicholson: *The Goddess Re-awakening: The Feminine*

Principle Today, Theosophical Publishing House, New York, 1989; Monica Sjöö & Barbara Mor, op.cit.; Edward C. Whitmont: *Return of the Goddess*, Routledge, 1987; Barbara G. Walker: *The Woman's Encyclopædia of Myths and Secrets*, Harper & Row, San Francisco, 1983; Lawrence Durdin-Robertson: *The Year of the Goddess*, Aquarian Press, 1990.

7. Z. Budapest, *The Book of Women's Mysteries*, Susan B. Anthony Coven, Oakland, CA, 1986, I, 3.

8. Coleridge: 'Christabel', quoted in J. Robinson, *Blinded By Her Light*, 60.

9. *Carmina Burana*, A. Hilka & O. Schumann, 1930, 168.

10. Sordello, in A. Press, 243.

11. In Wallis Budge, *The Gods of the Egyptians*, Dover Publications, New York, 1969, I, 380.

CHAPTER FOUR

1. Ovid, II, 1513; in B. O'Donoghue, 31.

2. Guido Guinicelll, in P. Dronke, *The Medieval Lyric*, 156.

3. M. Valency, 227, 270.

4. M. Foucault, 14.

5. G. Cavalcanti, in G.R. Ceriello, *I Rimatoria del dolce stil novo*, Milan 1950, 63.

6. Luigi Valli: *Il linguaggio segreto de Dante e dei fedeli d'anore*, Rome, 1928.

CHAPTER FIVE

1. In Dante Gabriel Rossetti: *The Early Italian Poets*, 97.

2. George Holmes: *Dante*, 15.

3. Francesco Petrarch, in T. Griffith, *Petrarch*, 25.

4. On the historical Laura, see Ernest Carra: "La leggenda di Laura", *Studi petrarcheschi e altri scritti*, Turin, 1959, 77-111.

5. Francesco Petrarch, letter to Giacomo Colonna, *Epistolæ metricæ*, in *Poemata minora*, 1, 6.

6. Tertullian, *Disciplinary, Moral and Ascetical Works*, tr. Rudolph Arbessman, Joseph Daly, New York, 1959.

7. John Chrystoston: *To the Fallen Monk Theodore*, in Herbert A. Masur, *Symbolism and the Christian Imagination*, Baltimore, 1962, 65f.

8. See Andrea Dworkin: *Pornography: Men Possessing Women*.

9. Marina Warner: *Alone of All Her Sex*, 126.

10. In T. Griffith, 23-4; Ernest Wilkins: *Life of Petrarch*, 77.

11. In Francesco Petrarch: *Selections from the Canzoniere*, tr. Mark Musa, 2.

12. *Secretum*, in Morris Bishop: *Petrarch and His World*, 203.

13. G. Guinicelli, in *Rimatori del dolce stil novo,* Luigi Dl Bendetto, Scrittori d'Italia, Bari, 1939.

CHAPTER SIX

1. Jalal al-Din Rumi: *Mathnawi*, in R.A. Nicholson, *Rumi*, 1956.

2. Al-Nuri, in Kalabadhi: *Al-Ta'amf,* 96, in A.J. Arberry: *Sufism.*

3. John of the Cross, *Dark Night of the Soul*, tr. E.A. Peers, Doubleday, New York, 1959.

4. Jan van Ruysbroeck: *The Adornment of the Spiritual Marriage*, tr. Wynschek, Dutton, New York, 1916, 122.

5. Walter Hilton: *Scale of Perfection,* II, 24f; in Eric Colledge: *The Medieval Mystics of England,* 10, 62.

6. E. Wilkins, 21, 57-8.

7. Quoted in E. Wilkins, 58.

8. Nicholas Mann: *Petrarch*, 48.

9. In *Selections From the Canzoniere.* tr. Mark Musa. 2f.

10. Simone Martini: *The Annunciation*, Uffizi, Florence.

11. Bruce Cole: *Siennese Painting From Its Origins To the Fifteenth Century.* Harper & Row, New York, 1980, 87.

12. Noted in Nicholas Mann, 3.

13. *Famillarum rerum libri: Le familiari,* ed. V. Rossi, Florence, 1942, II, 9.

14. Certainly Petrarch knew how good he was as a poet.

15. Al-Ahnaf, in *Lyrics From Arabia*, ed. Ghazi A. Algosabi, Washington, 1986, 24.

16. Al-Ghazzali, quoted in Idries Shah: *The Way of the Sufi*, Octagon Press, 1980, 51f.

17. Quoted in Mark Musa's translation, 50.

18. Arnaut Daniel, in B. O'Donoghue, 141.

19. Castelloza, in Meg Bogin: *The Women Troubadours,* 121.

20. D.H. Lawrence: *Fantasia of the Unconscious*, Heinemann, 1961, 191f.

21. Elizabeth Browning: *Sonnets For the Portuguese*, in Helen Gardner: *The New Oxford Book of English Verse*, Clarendon Press, 1972, 631.

CHAPTER SEVEN

1. Jetsun Milarepa in John Ferguson: *An Illustrated Encyclopædia of Mysticism*, Thames & Hudson, 1976, 120.

2. Catullus, quoted in J. Robinson, *Blinded By Her Light*, 121.

3. *Epistolæ metricæ: Francisci Petrarchæ poemata minora*, II, 11.

4. Philo: 'The most productive of all numbers.' Quoted in J.C. Cooper: *An Illustrated Encyclopædia of Traditional Symbols*, 16.

5. See Mircea Eliade: *Patterns in Comparative Religion*.

6. See Marina Warner, 97-98.

7. 'Landscapes are symbolic', writes J.E. Cirlot in *A Dictionary of Symbols*, tr. J. Sage, Routledge, 1981, 173.

8 Francesco Petrarch: *De remediis utriusque fortunæ*, tr. Thomas Twyne as *Phisick Against Fortune*, 1579, quoted in M. Bishop, 92.

CHAPTER EIGHT

1. Ovid, *Metamorphoses,* I-IV, 97-89, lines 177-185.

2. Sara Mack, *Ovid,* Yale University Press, New Haven, 1988, 162-3.

3. See Sara Sturm-Maddox: *Petrarch's Metamorphoses*, 2.

4. See J.C. Cooper, 164.

5. Ovid, op.cit., 163-4.

6. Sara Sturm-Maddox, 24.

7. James Hall, *Dictionary of Subjects and Symbols In Art,* John Murray, 1984, 190.

8. In A. Pauphilet: *Poets et romanciers du Moyen Age*, 1952, 865f.

9. In B. O'Donoghue, 141; A. Press, 185.

CHAPTER NINE

1. *Epistolæ metricæ*, in *Poemata minora*, op.cit., II, 11.

2. See Robert Graves: *The White Goddess*, Faber, 1961, 12, 98-99; Weston La Barre: *The Ghost Dance*, 352: 'the shaman-artist creates his cult and his god'; Lilian Feder: *Ancient Myth and Modern Poetry*, Princeton University Press, New Jersey, 1971.

3. Samuel Beckett, *Disjecta: Miscellaneous Writings*, ed. Ruby Cohn, Calder, 1983, 68.

4. Rainer Maria Rilke, *The Notebooks of Malte Laurids Brigge,* in *Selected Poetry*, tr. Stephen Mitchell, Picador, 1987, 306.

5. Paul Valéry, "Mallarmé", in *An Anthology*, ed. J.R. Lawler, Routledge, 1977, 168-9.

6. In *Letters from Petrarch*, 1966.

7. Edgar Quintet, *Les revolutions de'Italle*, Paris, 1878, I, 188.

8. Adolfo Bartoli: *Storia delle Letturatua Italiana*, 283.

9. Critics who note the self-consciousness of Francesco Petrarch include Mark Musa, Sandra Bermann, Morris Bishop, Peter Hainsworth, Sara Sturm-Maddox, Thomas Bergin and Robert M. Durling.

10. C.P. Cavafy quoted in Robert Lidell: *Cavafy: a critical biography*, Duckworth, 1974, 207.

11. See Leonard Forster: *The Icy Fire*; E. Bigi: *Del Petrarca al Leopardi*, 1-14; D. Alonson: "La poesia del Petrarca e il petrarchismo", 73-120; M. Fubini: "Il Petrarca artefice?", 1-12; T. Griffith, 34-6; R. Durling, 11-18.

12. *Roman de la Rose*, Ste Genevieve Bibllotheque, Paris, MS 1126.

13. Roman d'Artus, 14th century, Carpentras, Bibliothéque Inguimbertine, MS 5403, fol. 7.

14. Giraut de Borneil, in B. O'Donoghue, 126-7.

15. Peter Dronke, *Medieval Latin*, 67.

16. Andrea Capellanus, in Kenhelm Foster, *The Two Dantes*, 28.

17. A.J. Denomy, *Medieval Studies*, vol. 6 & 7, 1945; vol. 8, 1946, vol. 11, 1949.

18. Countess of Dis, in Meg Bogin, 89.

19. In C. von Kraus, *Minnesangs Frühling*, 1944, 141, 37.

20. In C. Appel, no. 39; in A. Press, 81.

21. See Alfred Jeanroy: *La Poesie lyrique des troubadours*; Denis de Rougemont: *Love in the Western World*, 1974; and Robert Briffault: *The Troubadours.*

22. In G. Gontini, *Poeti*, II, 555.

23. Claude Marks: *Pilgrims, Heretics and Lovers*, Macmillan, New York, 1975, x.

24. See Sybil Marksen: *La Femme au moyen-âge*, Edition Leipzig, Leipzig, 1974, 9.

25. Polly Toynbee: "Opinion", *Radio Times*, 5-11, December, 1992, 22.

26. Quoted in Dante Gabriel Rossetti, *The Early Italian Poets*, 61.

27. Powerful women in the mediæval era include: Loba de Pennautler, of the Carcassone region; the Viscountess Ermengarde of Narbonne (d. 1182); Agnes of Burgundy; Eleanor of Aquitaine; Blanche of Castile; and Marie de Chaoyagne (d. 1198).

28. See Marina Warner, op. cit., 144; Steven Runciman: *The Medieval Manichee: A Study of the Christian Dualist Heresy*, Cambridge, 1947.

29. F. Petrarch: *Triumph of Eternity*, in E. Wilkins, 245.

30. Jalal al-Din Rumi: *Selected Poems From the Divan*, Cambridge, 1898, 137.

31. St Bernard: *Sermons On the Song of Songs,* in F.C. Happold, *Mysticism,* 239.

32. Bernard Lonergan: *A Third Collection,* Paulist Press, New York, 1985, 133.

33. Francesco Petrarch, letter to Luca Cristian, 1349, *Epistolæ familliaræ,* tr. A.S. Bernardo, Albany, New York, 1975, VIII, 3.

34. In *De remediis utriusque fortunæ,* in *Francisci Petrarchæ opera,* Basle, 1554, II; in N. Mann, 82.

35. In *Familliares* XXIV, *Le faniliari,* e. V. Rossi, Florence, 1942.

36. *De remediis utriusque fortunæ,* op.cit., I, 69.

37. *The Secretum* in Morris Bishop, 204-7.

38. Dante Alighieri: *Literature In the Vernacular*, 40.

39. *Letter To Posterity,* in *Selections From the Canzoniere,* 1.

40. Francesco Petrarch: *De Otio religioso,* de Giuseppe Rotondi, 1958, 24-25.

41. See Eugene Vance: "Augustine's Confessions and the Grammar of Selfhood", in *Genre,* 6, 1973, 18-22; and S. Sturm-Maddox, op.cit.

42. Sandra Berman, 27.

43. *The Bhagavad-Gita,* 9.19f, 11.37f, in F.C. Happold, 157; see also R.C. Zaehner: *Mysticism Sacred and Profane,* 1957, 145f.

44. Meister Eckhart: *Sermons,* XCIX, tr. E. de B. Evans, in F.C. Happold, 273.

APPENDIX: ON PETRARCHISM

1. J.H. Whitfield: *A Short History of Italian Literature*, Penguin, 1960, 27.

2. On the influence of Petrarch in Britain, George Watson writes:

> It is probably significant that, of the two hundred or more editions (of the *Rime Sparse*) known to have appeared throughout Europe by 1600, not one was published in England. (*The English Petrarchans*)

3. Sappho, in David A. Campbell: *The Themes of the Greek Lyric Poets,* Duckworth, 1883, 17.

4. Maurice Scève: *The 'Delie' of Maurice Scève,* ed. I.D,. McFarlane, 1966; and see Dorothy Gabe Coleman: *Maurice Scève: Poet of Love: Tradition and Originality,* Cambridge University Press. 1975.

5. T. Tasso, in *The Penguin Book of Italian Verse,* ed. George Kay, 180.

6. P. Ronsard: *Les Amours,* in Stephen Minta, 166.

7. Giovanni Battista Marino: 'In Constant Love', in ib., 225.

8. M. Spiller, 87; Anne Ferry: *The 'Inward' Language,* Chicago 1983, chapter 2.

BIBLIOGRAPHY

FRANCESCO PETRARCH

Petrarch's Lyric Poems: The Rime Sparse and Other Lyrics, tr. Robert M. Durling, Harvard University Press, Cambridge, Mass, 1976

Selected Poems, ed. T. Gwynfor Griffith & P.R.J. Hainsworth, Manchester University Press, 1971

Selected Poems, tr. Anthony Mortimer, University of Alabama Press, Alabama, 1977

Selections From the 'Canzoniere' and Other Works, tr. Mark Musa, Oxford University Press, 1985

The Life of Solitude, tr. J. Zeitlin, Urbana, Illinois, 1924

Epistolæ metricæ: Francisci Petrarchæ poemata minora, ed. D. Rossetti, Milan, 1834

Letters From Petrarch, ed. Morris Bishop, Indiana University Press, Bloomington, 1966

Collected Works, vol. 1, by J.M. Synge, ed. Robin Skelton, Oxford University Press, 1962

ON PETRARCH

D. Alonson. "La poesia del Petrarca e il petrarehismo", *Studi petrarcheschi*, VII, 1961

T. Bahti. "Petrarch and the Scene of Writing: A Reading of *Rime* CXXIX", *Yale Italian Studies*, 1, 1980

—. *Ends of the Lyric: Direction and Consequence in Western Poetry*, Johns Hopkins University Press, Baltimore, MD, 1996

T. Barolini. "The Making of a Lyric Sequence: Time and Narrative in Petrarch's *Rerum vulgarium fragmenta*", *Modern Language Notes*, 104,

1989

Adolfo Bartoli. *Storia delle Letturatua Italiana*, from *Petrarca*, vol. VIII, Florence, 1884

Thomas Bergin. *Petrarch*, Twayne Publishers, Boston, 1970

A. Bernardo. "The importance of the non-love poems in Petrarch's *Canzoniere*", *Italica*, 27, 1950

—. "Petrarch and the Art of Literature", in J.A. Molinaro, 1973

—. *Petrarch, Laura, and the 'Triumphs'*, Albany, NY, 1974

—. ed. *Francesco Petrarca*, Albany, NY, 1980

—. & A.L. Pellegrini, eds. *Dante, Petrarch, Boccaccio, Medieval and Renaissance Texts and Studies*, Binghamton, 1983

E. Bigi. "Alcuni aspetti dello stile del *Canzoniere* petrarchesco", *Dal Petrarca al Leopardi*, Milan, 1954

—. "La rima del Petrarca", *Studi petrarcheschi*, 7, 1961

—. "La ballate del Petrarca", *Giornale storico della letteratura italiana*, 151, 1974

Morris Bishop. *Petrarch and His World*, Chatto & Windus, 1964

E.L. Boggs. "Cino and Petrarca", *Modern Language Notes*, 94, 1979

U. Bosco. *Francesco Petrarca*, Bari, 1961

M. O'Rouke Boyle. *Petrarch's Genius: Pentimento and Prophecy*, University of California Press, Berkeley, CA, 1991

G. Braden. "Love and Fame: The Petrarchan Career", in J. Smith, 1986

J. Brenkman. "Writing, Desire, Dialectic in Petrarch's *Rime* 23", *Pacific Coast Philology*, 9, 1974

G.A. Cesareo. *Su le 'poesie volgari' del Petrarca*, Rocca San Casciano, 1898

E. Chiappelli. *Studi sui linguaggio del Petrarca: la canzone della visioni*, Florence, 1971

G. Cipolla. "Labyrinthine Imagery in Petrarch", *Italica*, 54, 1977

R.J. Clements. "Préhistoire de l'aura de Pétraque", in *Varianti e altra linguistica*, 193-9, Einaudi, Turin, 1970

G. Contini. "Anti-Petrarchism of the Pléiade", *Modern Philology*, 39, 1942

Convegno Internazionale Francesco Petrarca, Rome, 1976

K. Cool. "The Petrarchan Landscape as Palimpsest", *Journal of Medieval and Renaissance Studies*, 11, 1981

M. Cottino-Jones. "The Myth of Apollo and Daphne in Petrarch's *Canzoniere*", in A. Scaglione, 1975

D. Dtuschke. *Francesco Petrarca: Canzone XXIII From First to Final Version*, Ravenna, 1977

—. "The Anniversary Poems in Petrarch's *Canzoniere*", *Italica*, 58, 1981

Heather Dubrow. *Echoes of Desire: English Petrarchism and Its Counterdiscourses*, Cornell University Press, 1995

R.M. Durling. "Petrarch's 'Giovene donna sotto un verde lauro'", *Modern Language Notes*, 86, 1971

L. Enterline. "Embodied Voices: Petrarch Reading (Himself Reading) Ovid", in V. Finucci, 1994

F. Figurelli. "L'architettura del sonetto in Francesco Petrarca", *Studi petrarcheschi*, 7, 1961

L.W. Foster. *The Icy Fire: Five Studies in European Petrarchism*, Cambridge University Press, 1969

J. Freccero. "The Fig Tree and the Laurel: Petrarch's Poetics", *Diacritics*, Spring, 1975

M. Fubini. "Il Petrarca artefice?", *Studi sulle letteratura de l'Rinascimento*, Florence, 1947, 1-12

G. Genot. "Petrarque et la scene du regard", *Journal of Medieval and Renaissance Studies*, 2, 1972

E. Gianturco. "The Double Gift: Inner Vision and Pictorial Sense in Petrarch", *Renaissance and Reformation*, 8, 1972

Roland Greene. *Post-Petrarchism: Origins and Innovations of the Western Lyric Sequence*, Princeton University Press, Princeton, 1991

P. Hainsworth. *Petrarch the Poet: An Introduction to the 'Rerum Vulgarium Fragmente'*, Routledge, London, 1988

F.J. Jones. "Laura's date of birth and the calendrical system implicit in the *Canzoniere*", *Italianistica*, 1, 1983

—. "Arguments in favour of a calendrical structure for Petrarch's *Canzoniere*", *Modern Language Review*, 79, 1984

—. "Further evidence of the identity of Petrarch's Laura", *Italian Studies*, 39, 1984

W.J. Kennedy. "Petrarchan Textuality", in M. Brownlee, 1989

Nicholas Mann. *Petrarch*, Oxford University Press, 1984

H.A. Mathes. "Petrarch's Tranquillo Porto'", *Italica*, 26, 1949

G. Mazzotta. "The *Canzoniere* and the Language of the Self", *Studies in Philology*, 75, 1978

—. "Petrarch's Song 126", in M.A. Caws, 1986

—. ed. *The World of Petrarch*, Duke University Press, Durham, NC, 1993

Petrarch and Petrarchism, tr. Stephen Minta, Manchester University Press, 1980

Julius A. Molinaro, ed. *Petrarch to Pirandello*, University of Toronto Press, Toronto, 1973

M. Perugi. *Trovatori a Valchiusa: un frammento della cultura provenzale del Petrarca*, Studi sul Petrarca, 18, Antenore, Padua, 1985

P. Possiedi. "Petrarca Petrosco", *Forum italicum*, 8, 1974

A.E. Quaglio. *Francesco Petrarca*, Milan, 1967

M.S. Regan. "Petrarch's Courtly and Christian Vocabularies: Language in *Canzoniere* 61-63", *Romance Notes*, 15, 1974

F. Rigolot. "Nature and Function of Paronomasia in the *Canzoniere*", *Italian Quarterly*, 18, 1974

T. Roche. "The Calendrical Structure of Petrarch's *Canzoniere*", *Studies in Philology*, 7, 1974

—. *Petrarch and the English Sonnet Sequences*, AMS Press, New York, 1989

N. Rosenberg. "Petrarch's Limping: The Foot Unequal to the Eye", *Modern Language Notes*, 77, 1962

A. Scaglione, ed. *Francis Petrarch: Six Centuries Later*, Chicago University Press, 1975

I. Scarano, ed. *Francesco Petrarca*, Naples, 1972

F. Schalk, ed. *Petrarca 1304-1374: Beitrage zu Werk und Wirkung*, Frankfurt, 1975

M. Shapiro. *Hieroglyph of Time: The Petrarchan Sestina*, Minneapolis, MN, 1980

B.T. Sozzi. *Petrarca*, Palermo, 1963

S. Sturm-Maddox. "Petrarch's Serpent in the Grass: The Fall as Subtext in the *Rime Sparse*", *Journal of Medieval and Renaissance Studies*, 13, 1983

—. *Petrarch's Metamorphoses: Text and Subtext in the Rime Sparse*, University of Missouri Press, Columbia, 1985

—. "Petrarch's Siren", *Italian Quarterly*, 103, 1986

J. Tilden. "Spiritual Conflict in Petrarch's *Canzoniere*", in F. Schalk

Charles Trinkaus. *The Poet as Philosopher: Petrarch and the Foundation of Renaissance Consciousness*, Yale University Press, New Haven, 1979

M. Turchi. "Il centenario del Petrarca e la critica", *Italianistica*, 7, 1978

G. Velli. "La memoria poetica del Petrarca", *Italia medievale e umanistica*, 19, 1976

—. "La metafora del Petrarca", in D. Goldin, 1980

M. Waller. *Petrarch's Poetics and Literary History*, Amherst, MA, 1980

G. Watson. *Petrarch and the English*, Yale University Press, 1979

—. *The English Petrarchans*, Warburg Institute, London, 1992

E.H. Wilkins. *The Making of the 'Canzoniere' and other Petrarchan Studies*, Rome, 1951

—. *Studies In the Life and Works of Petrarch*, Harvard University Press, Cambridge, MA, 1955

—. *Petrarch At Vaucluse*, Chicago University Press, Chicago, IL, 1958

—. *Petrarch's Eight Years In Milan*, Harvard University Press, Cambridge, MA, 1958

—. *Petrarch's Later Years*, Harvard University Press, Cambridge, MA, 1959

—. *Petrarch's Correspondence*, Harvard University Press, Cambridge, MA, 1960

—. *Life of Petrarch*, Chicago University Press, Chicago, IL, 1961

E. Williamson. "A Consideration of 'Virgine bella'", *Italica*, 29, 1952

DANTE ALIGHIERI

Rime della 'Vita Nuova' e della giovinezza, eds. M. Barbi & F. Maggini, Le Monnier, Florence, 1956

Le Opere di Dante Alighieri, ed. E. Moore, Oxford University Press, 1963

Dante's Lyric Poetry, ed. K. Foster & P. Boyde, Oxford University Press, 1967

Dante: Literature in the Vernacular, tr. Sally Purcell, Carcanet Press, Manchester, 1981

The Divine Comedy, 3 vols, vol. III, *Paradise*, tr. Mark Musa, Penguin, 1986

The Divine Comedy, tr. Lawrence Binyon, Agenda, 1979

Vita Nuova, tr. Mark Musa, Oxford University Press, 1992

The Portable Dante, ed. Mark Musa, Penguin, 1995

ON DANTE

Richard Abrams. "Illicit Pleasures: Dante Among the Sensualists", *Modern Language Notes*, 100, 1985

William Anderson. *Dante the Maker*, Hutchinson, 1983

J.A. Barber. "The Role of the Other in Dante's *Vita Nuova*", *Studies in Philology*, 78, 1981

Teodolinda Barolini. *The Undivine "Comedy", Dethroning Dante*, Princeton University Press, 1992

Thomas Bergin, ed. *From Time To Eternity*, Yale University Press, New Haven, 1967

—. *A Diversity of Dante*, Rutgers University Press, New Brunswick, 1969

—. *Dante's Divine Comedy*, Prentice-Hall, New Jersey, 1971

Dino Bigongiari. "Dante's *Vita Nuova*" in *Essays on Dante and Medieval Culture*, Olshki, Florence, 1964

Harold Bloom, ed. *Dante*, Chelsea House, New York, 1986

Umberto Bosco. *Handbook to Dante Studies*, Oxford, 1950

—. ed. *Enciclopedia dantesca*, 6 vols, Instituto dell'Enciclopedia Italiana, 1970-78

C.M. Bowra. *Inspiration and Poetry*, Macmillan, 1955

Patrick Boyde, *Dante's Style in His Lyric Poetry*, Cambridge University Press, 1971

Marina S. Brownlee *et al*, eds. *The New Medievalism*, John Hopkins University Press, Baltimore, 1991

Michael Caesar, ed. *Dante: The Critical Heritage 1314(?)-1870*, Routledge, 1989

M. Carruthers. *The Book of Memory: A Study of Memory in Medieval Culture*, Olschki, Florence, 1964

Dino Cervigni. *Dante's Poetry of Dreams*, Olschki, Florence, 1986

—. ed. *Dante and Modern American Criticism*, *Annalis d'Italianistica*, 8, 1990

R.J. Clements, ed. *Dante: A Collection of Critical Essays*, New Jersey, 1965

Stelio Cro. "*Vita Nuova* figura *Comoediæ*: Dante tra la Villana Morte e Matelda", *Italian Culture*, 6, 1985

Antonio D'Andrea. "La struttura della *Vita Nuova*: Le divisioni delle rime", *Yearbook of Italian Studies*, 4, 1980

Robert M. Durling & Ronald L. Martinez. *Time and the Crystal: Studies in Dante's 'Rime Petrose'*, University of California Press, Berkeley, 1990

Gerda Elata-Aster. "Gathering the Leaves and Squaring the Circle: *Recording, Reading* and *Writing* in Dante's *Vita Nuova* and *Divina Commedia*", *Italian Quarterly*, 24, 92, 1983

Francois Ferguson. *Dante*, Weidenfeld & Nicolson, 1966

J.B. Fletcher. *Dante*, Notre Dame University Press, 1965

—. "The True Meaning of Dante's *Vita Nuova*", *Romanic Review*, 11, 1920

Kenhelm Foster. "The Mind in Love: Dante's Philosophy", in J. Freccero, 1965

—. & Patrick Boyde, ed. *Dante's Lyric Poetry*, Oxford University Press, 1967

—. "Dante's Idea of Love", in T. Bergin, 1967

—. *The Two Dantes and Other Studies*, Darton, Longman, Todd, 1977

W. Franke. *Dante's Interpretive Journey*, Chicago University Press, 1996

John Freccero, ed. *Dante: A Collection of Critical Essays*, Prentice-Hall, Englewood Cliffs, 1965

—. "Dante's Medusa: Allegory and Autobiography", in D. Jeffrey, 1979

—. ed. *Dante: The Poetics of Conversion*, Harvard University Press, Cambridge, Mass., 1986

Edmund Gardner. *Dante's Ten Heavens*, New York, 1970

John Guzzardo. "Number Symbolism in the *Vita Nuova*", *Canadian Journal of Italian Studies*, 8, 30, 1985

Robert P. Harrison. *The Body of Beatrice*, John Hopkins University Press, Baltimore, 1988

—. *Forests: The Shadow of Civilization*, University of Chicago Press, IL, 1992

Robert Hollander. "*Vita Nuova*: Dante's Perceptions of Beatrice", *Dante Studies*, 92, 1974

Julia B. Holloway. "The *Vita Nuova*: Paradigms of Pilgrimage", *Studies*, 103, 1985

George Holmes. *Dante*, Oxford University Press, 1980

Kay Howe. "Dante's Beatrice: The Nine and the Ten", *Italica*, 52, 1975

Amilcare A. Ianucci, ed. *Dante Today, Quaderni d'Italianistica*, 10, nos. 1-2, 1989

—. ed. *Dante: Contemporary Perspectives*, Toronto, 1995

Rachel Jacoff. "The Tears of Beatrice", *Dante Studies*, C, 1982

—. "Transgression and Transcendence: Figures of Female Desire in Dante's *Commedia*", in M. Brownlee, 1991

—. ed. *The Cambridge Companion to Dante*, Cambridge University Press, 1993

D.L. Jeffrey, ed. *By Things Seen: Reference and Recognition in Medieval Thought*, Ottawa, 1979

Robin Kirkpatrick. *Dante's Inferno: Difficulty and Dead Poetry*, Cambridge University Press, 1987

—. "Dante and the Body", in Kay, 1996

J. Kleiner. "Finding the Center: Revelation and Reticence in the *Vita Nuova*", *Texas Studies in Literature and Language*, 32, 1, 1980

P.J. Klemp. "The Woman in the Middle: Layers of Love in Dante's *Vita Nuova*", *Italia*, 61, 3, 1984

Jerome Mazzaro. *The Figure of Dante: An Essay on the 'Vita Nuova'*, Princeton University Press, 1981

Joseph A. Mazzeo. "Dante's Sun Symbolism", *Italica*, 33, Dec, 1956

—. *Medieval Cultural Tradition in Dante's 'Comedy'*, Cornell University Press, Ithaca, 1960

Guiseppe Mazzotta. *Dante, Poet of the Desert: History and Allegory in 'The Divine Comedy'*, Princeton University Press, 1979

—. "The Language of Poetry in the *Vita Nuova*", *Revisita di studi italini*, 1, 1983

—. ed. *Critical Essays on Dante*, Hall, Boston, 1991

—. *Dante's Vision and the Circle of Knowledge*, Princeton University Press, 1992

Antonio C. Mastrobuono. *Dante's Journey of Sanctification*, Regnery Gateway, Washington DC, 1990

K. McKenzie. "The Symbolic Structure of Dante's *Vita Nuova*", *PMLA*, 18, 1903

Vincent Moleta. "The *Vita Nuova* as a Lyric Narrative", *Forum Italicum*, 12, 1978

Edward Moore. *Studies in Dante*, ed. Colin Hardie, 4 vols, Oxford University Press, 1968

Alison Morgan. *Dante and the Medieval Other World*, Cambridge University Press, 1990

Mark Musa. *Essays on Dante*, Indiana University Press, Bloomington, 1964

—. *Dante's* Vita Nuova: *A Translation and an Essay*, Indiana University Press, Bloomington, 1973

—. *Advent at the Gates: Dante's Comedy*, Indiana University Press, Bloomington, 1974

Barbara Nolan. "The *Vita Nuova*: Dante's Book of Revelation", *Dante Studies*, 88, 1970

David Nolan, ed. *Dante Commentaries*, New Jersey, 1977

Charles Eliot Norton. *The New Life of Dante Alighieri*, Houghton-Mifflin, Boston 1895

Michelangelo Picone. "Strutture poetiche e strutture prosastiche nella *Vita Nuova*", *Modern Language Notes*, 92, 1977

—. "*Vita Nuova*" *e tradizione romanza*, Liviana Editrice, Padua, 1979

Arshi Pipa. "Personaggi della *Vita Nuova*: Dante, Cavalcanti e la famiglia Portinari", *Italica*, 62, 2, 1985

J.H. Potter. "Beatrice Dead or Alive: Love in the *Vita Nuova*", *Texas Studies in Literature and Language*, 32, 1990

Ricardo Quinones. *Dante Alighieri*, Twayne, Boston, 1979

Domenico De Roberts, ed. *Vita Nuova*, Riccardo Ricciardi, Milan, 1980

—. *Il libro della* Vita Nuova, Sansoni, Florence, 1970

J.A. Scott. "Dante's 'Sweet New Style' and the *Vita Nuova*", *Italica*, 42, 1965

—. *Woman Earthly and Divine in the Comedy of Dante*, Lexington, 1975

Charles Singleton. *An Essay on the Vita Nuova*, Harvard University Press, Cambridge, Mass., 1949/ 1977

—. *Dante's 'Commedia': Elements of Structure*, Dante Studies 1, Harvard University Press, Cambridge, Mass., 1954

—. *Journey To Beatrice*, Dante Studies 2, Harvard University Press, Cambridge, Mass., 1958

Janet L. Smarr. "Celestial Patterns and Symmetries in the *Vita Nuova*", *Dante Studies*, 98, 1980

B. Stambler. *Dante's Other World*, New York University Press, 1957

Sara Sturm-Maddox. "The Pattern of Witness: Narrative Design in the *Vita Nuova*", *Forum Italicum*, 12, 1978

—. "Transformations of Courtly Poetry: *Vita Nuova* and *Canzoniere*", in J. Smith, 1980

Margherita De Bonfils Templer. *Itinerario di Amore: Dialettica di Amore e Morte nella* Vita Nuova, University of North Carolina Studies in Romance Languages and Literatures, Chapel Hill, 1973

David Thompson. *Dante's Epic Journeys,* John Hopkins University Press, Baltimore, 1974

J.F. Took. *Dante, Lyric Poet and Philosopher: An Introduction to the Minor Works*, Oxford University Press, 1990

Nancy J. Vickers. "Diana described: scattered woman and scattered rhymes", *Critical Enquiry*, 8, 1981

Michel J. Viegnes. "Space and Love in the *Vita Nuova*", *Lectura Dantis*, 4, 1989

E.R. Vincent. "The Crisis in the *Vita Nuova*", *Century Essays on Dante by Members of the Oxford Dante Society*, Clarendon Press, 1965

David Wallace, ed. *Texas Studies in Literature and Language*, Spring, 1990

ON DANTE AND PETRARCH

Aldo Bernardo, ed. "Petrarch's attitude towards Dante", *Proceedings of the Modern Language Association*, 70, 1955

G. Billanovich. "Tra Dante e Petrarca", *Italia medievale e umanistica*, 8, 1965

Michele Feo. "Petrarca e Dante", *Enciclopedia Dantesca*, 4, 1973

J. Larner. *Italy in the Age of Dante and Petrarch*, London, 1980

A. Moschetti. *Dell' Inspirazione dantesca nelle Rime di Francesco Petrarca*, Urbana, 1894

A.L. Pellegrini, eds. *Dante, Petrarch, Boccaccio, Medieval and Renaissance Texts and Studies*, Binghamton, 1983

M. Santagata. "Presenze di Dante 'comico' nel 'Canzoniere' del Petrarca", *Giornale storic della letteratura italiana*, 146, 1969

—. *Dal sonetto al canzoniere*, Padua, 1979

F. Suitner. *Petrarca e la tradizione stilnovistica*, Florence, 1977

P. Trovato. *Dante in Petrarca: Per un inventario dei dantismi nei Rerum Vulgarium Fragmente*, Florence, 1979

ON DANTE AND ARNAUT DANIEL

Ronald L. Martinez. "Dante Embarks Arnaut", *NEMLA Italian Studies*, 15, 1991

Elio Melli. "Dante e Arnaut Daniel", *Filologia romanza*, 6, 1959

Maurizio Perugi. "Dante e Arnaut Daniel", *Studi Danteschi*, 51, 1978

—. "Il Sordello di Dante e la tradizione mediolatina dell'invettiva", *Studi danteschi*, 55, 1983

Maria Picchio Simonelli. "La sestina Dantesca fra Arnaut Daniel e il Petrarca", *Dante Studies*, 91, 1973

ON DANTE AND THE TROUBADOURS

Thomas Bergin. "Dante's Provençal Gallery", *Speculum*, 40, 1965

Henry Chaytor. *The Troubadours of Dante*, Oxford University Press, 1902

Peter Hainsworth. "Cavalcanti in the *Vita Nuova*", *Modern Language Review*, 83, 1988

Klaus Kropfinger. "Dante e l'arte dei trovatori", in Pestalozza, 1988

Ronald L. Martinez. "Dante and the Two Canons", *Comparative Literature Studies*, 32, 1955

James V. Mirollo. "In Praise of Labella mano: Aspects of Late Renaissance Lyricism", *Comparative Literature Studiesø*, 9, 1972

Michelangelo Picone. "La *Vita Nuova* e la tradizone poetica", *Dante Studies*, 95, 1977

—. "I travatori di Dante: Bertran de Born", *Studi e problemi di critica testuale*, 19, 1979

—. "Giraut de Bornelh nella prospettiva di Dante", *Vox Romanica*, 39, 1980

F. Pirot. "Dante et les troubadours", *Marche romane*, 15, 1965

TROUBADOURS

Anthology of Troubadour Lyric Poetry, ed. Alan R. Press, Edinburgh University Press, 1971

The Courtly Love Tradition, ed. Bernard O'Donoghue, Manchester University Press, 1982

ON THE TROUBADOURS

F.R.P. Akehurst. "Words and Acts in the Troubadours", in M. Lazar, 1989
C. Appel. *Bernart von Ventadorn*, Halle a.S., 1915
R. Boase. *The Origin and Meaning of Courtly Love*, Manchester University Press, 1977
Meg Bogin, *The Women Troubadours*, Paddington Press, New York, 1976
Robert Briffault, *The Troubadours*, ed. L.F. Koons, Indiana University Press, Bloomington, 1965
A.J. Denomy. "Fin' Amors: The Pure Love of the Troubadours, Its Amorality and Possible Source", *Medieval Studies*, VII, 1945
—. *The Heresy of Courtly Love*, New York, 1947
—. "Jois Among the Early Troubadours", *Medieval Studies*, 13, 1951
Alfred Jeanroy. *Les Chansons de Guillaune IX*, Due d'Aquitaine, Paris, 1927
—. *La Poesie lyrique des troubadours*, Didler-Privat, Paris, 1934
Laura Kendrick. *The Game of Love: Troubadour Wordplay*, University of California, Los Angeles, 1988
Christopher Kleinhenz. *The Early Italian Sonnet: The First Century (1220-1321)*, Milella, Lecce, 1986
Jack Lindsay. *The Troubadours and Their World*, Frederick Mueller, 1976
Ulrich Mölk. *Trobar clus, trobar leu*, Fink, Munich, 1968
F.X. Newman, ed. *The Meaning of Courtly Love*, State University of New York Press, Albany, New York, 1968
W.D. Paden. "The Troubadour's Lady", *Studies in Philology*, 72, 1975
Linda M. Paterson. *Troubadours and Eloquence*, Oxford University Press, 1975
W.T. Pattison, *The Life and Works of the Troubadour Raimbaut d'Orange*, Minnesota, 1952
G. Toja. *Arnaut Daniel's Canzoni*, Florence, 1960
L.T. Topsfleld. *Troubadours and Love*, Cambridge University Press, 1975

OTHERS

A.J. Arberry, *Sufism*, Allen & Unwin, 1979
Geoffrey Ashe. *The Virgin*, Routledge, 1987
Sandra L. Berman. *The Sonnet Over Time; A Study In the Sonnets of Petrarch, Shakespeare and Baudelaire*, University of North Carolina, Chapel Hill, 1988
Joseph Campbell. *The Power of Myth*, Doubleday, New York, 1988

Andreas Capellanus. *The Art of Courtly Love,* Manchester University Press, 1961

M.A. Caws. *Some Readers Reading,* New York, NY, 1986

J.C. Cooper. *An Illustrated Encyclopædia of Traditional Symbols,* Thames & Hudson, 1982

Dionysus the Areopagite. *The Mystical Theology* and *The Celestial Hierarchies,* tr. Editors of the Shrine of Wisdom, Surrey, England, 1965

Peter Dronke. *Medieval Latin and the Rise of the European Love-Lyric,* Oxford University Press, 1968

—. *The Medieval Lyric,* Hutchinson, 1968

Andrea Dworkin. *Pornography: Men Possessing Women,* Women's Press, 1981

Mircea Eliade. *Patterns In Comparative Religion,* Sheed & Ward, 1958

—. *Shamanism,* Princeton University Press, New Jersey, 1972

—. *A History of Religious Ideas,* I, Collins, 1978

V. Finccucci. *Desire In the Renaissance,* Princeton University Press, 1994

Leonard Forster. *The Icy Fire,* Cambridge University Press, 1969

Michel Foucault, *The Use of Pleasure: The History of Sexuality,* vol. 2. tr. Robert Hurley, Penguin, 1987

D. Goldin, ed. *Simbolo, metafora, allegoria,* Padua, 1980

Christopher Hacker. *The History of Gardens,* Croom Helm, 1979

Peter Hainsworth *et al,* eds. *The Languages of Literature in Renaissance Italy,* Oxford University Press, 1988

F.C. Happold. *Mysticism,* Penguin, 1970

Robert Hollander. *Boccaccio's Two Venuses,* Columbia University Press, New York, 1977

George Kay, ed. *The Penguin Book of Italian Verse,* Penguin, 1965

Sarah Kay & Miri Rubin, eds. *Framing Medieval Bodies,* Manchester University Press, 1996

J. Kristeva. *Revolution in Poetic Language,* tr. Margaret Walker, Columbia University Press, New York, 1984

—. *The Kristeva Reader,* ed. Toril Moi, Blackwell, Oxford, 1986

—. *Tales of Love,* tr. Leon S. Roudiez, Columbia University Press, New York, N.Y., 1987

Margaret Wade Labarge. *Women In Medieval Life: A Small Sound of the Trumpet,* Hamish Hamilton, 1986

Weston La Barre. *The Ghost Dance,* Allen & Unwin, 1972

Moshe Lazar & Norris Lacy, eds. *The Poetics of Love in the Middle Ages: Texts and Contexts,* George Mason University Press, Fairfax, Va., 1989

C.S. Lewis. *The Allegory of Love,* Oxford University Press, 1951

J.P. Migne. *Patrilogiæ cursus completus,* Series Latina, Parisils, 1843-55

Edwin Morgan, ed. & tr. *Fifty Renascence Love-Poems*, Whiteknights Press, Reading, 1975

R.A. Nicholson. *Studies in Islamic Mysticism,*1921

Ovid. *Metamorphoses*, I-IV, tr. D.E. Hill, Arts & Phillips, Warminster, Wilts, 1985

Philip Rice & Patricia Waugh, eds. *Modern Literary Theory: A Reader*, Arnold, London, 1992

Dante Gabriel Rossetti. *The Early Italian Poets*, ed. Sally Purcell, Anvil Press Poetry, 1981

Denis de Rougemont. *Passion and Society*, tr. M. Belgion, 1940

—. *Love in the Western World*, Harper & Row, New York, 1974

Jeremy Robinson, *Blinded By Her Light: The Love-Poetry of Robert Graves*, Crescent Moon, 1991

J. Smith & W. Kerrigan, eds. *Pragmatism's Freud*, Johns Hopkins University Press, Batlimore, 1986

Michael R.G. Spiller. *The Development of the Sonnet: An Introduction*, Routledge, 1992

Stendhal. *De l'Amour*, tr. Sale, Penguin, 1975

Maurice Valency. *In Praise of Love: An Introduction to the Love-Poetry of the Renaissance*, Macmilllan, New York, 1961

Helen Waddell. *Medieval Latin Lyrics*, New York, 1953

Marina Warner. *Alone of All Her Sex: The Myth and Cult of the Virgin Mary*, Picador, 1985

WEBSITES

Good websites for Petrarch and Dante include:
• petrarch.petersadlon.com
• Petrarch at Penn Libraries
• Yale University
• Petrarch Forever at translation-ink.com
• greatdante.net
• Dante Digital Project

Arseny Tarkovsky

Life, Life

Selected Poems

Arseny Tarkovsky is the neglected Russian poet, father of the acclaimed film director Andrei Tarkovsky. This new book gathers together many of Tarkovsky's most lyrical and heartfelt poems, in Virginia Rounding's new, clear translations. Many of Tarkovsky's poems appeared in his son's films, such as *Mirror, Stalker, Nostalghia* and *The Sacrifice*. There is an introduction by Rounding, and a bibliography of both Arseny and Andrei Tarkovsky.

Illustrated. Bibliography and notes.
ISBN 9781816171144 Pbk   ISBN 9781861712660 Hbk

In the Dim Void

Samuel Beckett's Late Trilogy:
Company, Ill Seen, Ill Said and *Worstward Ho*

by Gregory Johns

This book discusses the luminous beauty and dense, rigorous poetry of Samuel Beckett's late works, *Company, Ill Seen, Ill Said* and *Worstward Ho*. Gregory Johns looks back over Beckett's long writing career, charting the development from the *Molloy-Malone Dies-Unnamable* trilogy through the 'fizzles' of the 1960s to the elegiac lyricism of the *Company* series. Johns compares the trilogy with late plays such as *Ghosts, Footfalls* and *Rockaby*.

Bibliography, notes. Illustrated. 120pp
ISBN 9781861712974 Pbk and ISBN 9781861712608 Hbk
9781861713407 E-book

Beauties, Beasts, and Enchantment

CLASSIC FRENCH FAIRY TALES

Translated and with an Introduction
by Jack Zipes

A collection of 36 classic French fairy tales translated by renowned writer Jack Zipes.
Cinderella, Beauty and the Beast, Sleeping Beauty and *Little Red Riding Hood* are among the classic fairy tales in this amazing book.
Includes illustrations from fairy tale collections.
Jack Zipes has written and published widely on fairy tales.

'Terrific... a succulent array of 17th and 18th century 'salon' fairy tales'
- *The New York Times Book Review*

'These tales are adventurous, thrilling in a way fairy tales are meant to be... The translation from the French is modern, happily free of archaic and hyperbolic language... a fine and sophisticated collection' - *New York Tribune*

'Enjoyable to read... a unique collection of French regional folklore' - *Library Journal*

'Charming stories accompanied by attractive pen-and-ink drawings' - *Chattanooga Times*

Introduction and illustrations 612pp. ISBN 9781861712510 Pbk ISBN 9781861713193 Hbk

CRESCENT MOON PUBLISHING

web: www.crmoon.com e-mail: cresmopub@yahoo.co.uk

ARTS, PAINTING, SCULPTURE

The Art of Andy Goldsworthy
Andy Goldsworthy: Touching Nature
Andy Goldsworthy in Close-Up
Andy Goldsworthy: Pocket Guide
Andy Goldsworthy In America
Land Art: A Complete Guide
The Art of Richard Long
Richard Long: Pocket Guide
Land Art In the UK
Land Art in Close-Up
Land Art In the U.S.A.
Land Art: Pocket Guide
Installation Art in Close-Up
Minimal Art and Artists In the 1960s and After
Colourfield Painting
Land Art DVD, TV documentary
Andy Goldsworthy DVD, TV documentary
The Erotic Object: Sexuality in Sculpture From Prehistory to the Present Day
Sex in Art: Pornography and Pleasure in Painting and Sculpture
Postwar Art
Sacred Gardens: The Garden in Myth, Religion and Art
Glorification: Religious Abstraction in Renaissance and 20th Century Art
Early Netherlandish Painting
Leonardo da Vinci
Piero della Francesca
Giovanni Bellini
Fra Angelico: Art and Religion in the Renaissance
Mark Rothko: The Art of Transcendence
Frank Stella: American Abstract Artist
Jasper Johns
Brice Marden
Alison Wilding: The Embrace of Sculpture
Vincent van Gogh: Visionary Landscapes
Eric Gill: Nuptials of God
Constantin Brancusi: Sculpting the Essence of Things
Max Beckmann
Caravaggio
Gustave Moreau
Egon Schiele: Sex and Death In Purple Stockings
Delizioso Fotografico Fervore: Works In Process 1
Sacro Cuore: Works In Process 2
The Light Eternal: J.M.W. Turner
The Madonna Glorified: Karen Arthurs

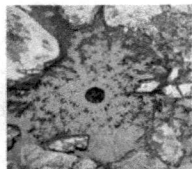

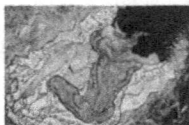

LITERATURE

J.R.R. Tolkien: The Books, The Films, The Whole Cultural Phenomenon
J.R.R. Tolkien: Pocket Guide
Tolkien's Heroic Quest
The *Earthsea* Books of Ursula Le Guin
Beauties, Beasts and Enchantment: Classic French Fairy Tales
German Popular Stories by the Brothers Grimm
Philip Pullman and *His Dark Materials*
Sexing Hardy: Thomas Hardy and Feminism
Thomas Hardy's *Tess of the d'Urbervilles*
Thomas Hardy's *Jude the Obscure*
Thomas Hardy: The Tragic Novels
Love and Tragedy: Thomas Hardy
The Poetry of Landscape in Hardy
Wessex Revisited: Thomas Hardy and John Cowper Powys
Wolfgang Iser: Essays and Interviews
Petrarch, Dante and the Troubadours
Maurice Sendak and the Art of Children's Book Illustration
Andrea Dworkin
Cixous, Irigaray, Kristeva: The *Jouissance* of French Feminism
Julia Kristeva: Art, Love, Melancholy, Philosophy, Semiotics and Psychoanalysis
Hélene Cixous I Love You: The *Jouissance* of Writing
Luce Irigaray: Lips, Kissing, and the Politics of Sexual Difference
Peter Redgrove: Here Comes the Flood
Peter Redgrove: Sex-Magic-Poetry-Cornwall
Lawrence Durrell: Between Love and Death, East and West
Love, Culture & Poetry: Lawrence Durrell
Cavafy: Anatomy of a Soul
German Romantic Poetry: Goethe, Novalis, Heine, Hölderlin
Feminism and Shakespeare
Shakespeare: Love, Poetry & Magic
The Passion of D.H. Lawrence
D.H. Lawrence: Symbolic Landscapes
D.H. Lawrence: Infinite Sensual Violence
Rimbaud: Arthur Rimbaud and the Magic of Poetry
The Ecstasies of John Cowper Powys
Sensualism and Mythology: The Wessex Novels of John Cowper Powys
Amorous Life: John Cowper Powys and the Manifestation of Affectivity (H.W. Fawkner)
Postmodern Powys: New Essays on John Cowper Powys (Joe Boulter)
Rethinking Powys: Critical Essays on John Cowper Powys
Paul Bowles & Bernardo Bertolucci
Rainer Maria Rilke
Joseph Conrad: *Heart of Darkness*
In the Dim Void: Samuel Beckett
Samuel Beckett Goes into the Silence
André Gide: Fiction and Fervour
Jackie Collins and the Blockbuster Novel
Blinded By Her Light: The Love-Poetry of Robert Graves
The Passion of Colours: Travels In Mediterranean Lands
Poetic Forms

POETRY

Ursula Le Guin: Walking In Cornwall
Peter Redgrove: Here Comes The Flood
Peter Redgrove: Sex-Magic-Poetry-Cornwall
Dante: Selections From the Vita Nuova
Petrarch, Dante and the Troubadours
William Shakespeare: Sonnets
William Shakespeare: Complete Poems
Blinded By Her Light: The Love-Poetry of Robert Graves
Emily Dickinson: Selected Poems
Emily Brontë: Poems
Thomas Hardy: Selected Poems
Percy Bysshe Shelley: Poems
John Keats: Selected Poems
Joh n Keats: Poems of 1820
D.H. Lawrence: Selected Poems
Edmund Spenser: Poems
Edmund Spenser: Amoretti
John Donne: Poems
Henry Vaughan: Poems
Sir Thomas Wyatt: Poems
Robert Herrick: Selected Poems
Rilke: Space, Essence and Angels in the Poetry of Rainer Maria Rilke
Rainer Maria Rilke: Selected Poems
Friedrich Hölderlin: Selected Poems
Arseny Tarkovsky: Selected Poems
Arthur Rimbaud: Selected Poems
Arthur Rimbaud: A Season in Hell
Arthur Rimbaud and the Magic of Poetry
Novalis: Hymns To the Night
German Romantic Poetry
Paul Verlaine: Selected Poems
Elizaethan Sonnet Cycles
D.J. Enright: By-Blows
Jeremy Reed: Brigitte's Blue Heart
Jeremy Reed: Claudia Schiffer's Red Shoes
Gorgeous Little Orpheus
Radiance: New Poems
Crescent Moon Book of Nature Poetry
Crescent Moon Book of Love Poetry
Crescent Moon Book of Mystical Poetry
Crescent Moon Book of Elizabethan Love Poetry
Crescent Moon Book of Metaphysical Poetry
Crescent Moon Book of Romantic Poetry
Pagan America: New American Poetry

MEDIA, CINEMA, FEMINISM and CULTURAL STUDIES

J.R.R. Tolkien: The Books, The Films, The Whole Cultural Phenomenon
J.R.R. Tolkien: Pocket Guide
The *Lord of the Rings* Movies: Pocket Guide
The Cinema of Hayao Miyazaki
Hayao Miyazaki: *Princess Mononoke*: Pocket Movie Guide
Hayao Miyazaki: *Spirited Away*: Pocket Movie Guide
Tim Burton : Hallowe'en For Hollywood
Ken Russell
Ken Russell: *Tommy*: Pocket Movie Guide
The Ghost Dance: The Origins of Religion
The Peyote Cult
Cixous, Irigaray, Kristeva: The *Jouissance* of French Feminism
Julia Kristeva: Art, Love, Melancholy, Philosophy, Semiotics and Psychoanalysis
Luce Irigaray: Lips, Kissing, and the Politics of Sexual Difference
Hélene Cixous I Love You: The *Jouissance* of Writing
Andrea Dworkin
'Cosmo Woman': The World of Women's Magazines
Women in Pop Music
HomeGround: The Kate Bush Anthology
Discovering the Goddess (Geoffrey Ashe)
The Poetry of Cinema
The Sacred Cinema of Andrei Tarkovsky
Andrei Tarkovsky: Pocket Guide
Andrei Tarkovsky: *Mirror*: Pocket Movie Guide
Andrei Tarkovsky: *The Sacrifice*: Pocket Movie Guide
Walerian Borowczyk: Cinema of Erotic Dreams
Jean-Luc Godard: The Passion of Cinema
Jean-Luc Godard: *Hail Mary*: Pocket Movie Guide
Jean-Luc Godard: *Contempt*: Pocket Movie Guide
Jean-Luc Godard: *Pierrot le Fou*: Pocket Movie Guide
John Hughes and Eighties Cinema
Ferris Bueller's Day Off: Pocket Movie Guide
Jean-Luc Godard: Pocket Guide
The Cinema of Richard Linklater
Liv Tyler: Star In Ascendance
Blade Runner and the Films of Philip K. Dick
Paul Bowles and Bernardo Bertolucci
Media Hell: Radio, TV and the Press
An Open Letter to the BBC
Detonation Britain: Nuclear War in the UK
Feminism and Shakespeare
Wild Zones: Pornography, Art and Feminism
Sex in Art: Pornography and Pleasure in Painting and Sculpture
Sexing Hardy: Thomas Hardy and Feminism

The Light Eternal is a model monograph, an exemplary job. The subject matter of the book is beautifully organised and dead on beam. (Lawrence Durrell)
It is amazing for me to see my work treated with such passion and respect. (Andrea Dworkin)

CRESCENT MOON PUBLISHING
P.O. Box 1312, Maidstone, Kent, ME14 5XU, Great Britain. www.crmoon.com

cresmopub@yahoo.co.uk   www.crescentmoon.org.uk

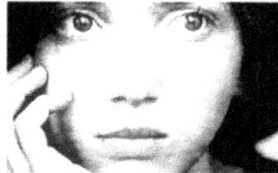